Joseph
Oklahoma
32751

9
Jy

DATE DUE

1998	

PRINTED IN U.S.A.

The United States

Oklahoma

Paul Joseph
ABDO & Daughters

visit us at
www.abdopub.com

Published by Abdo & Daughters, 4940 Viking Drive, Suite 622, Edina, Minnesota 55435.
Copyright © 1998 by Abdo Consulting Group, Inc., Pentagon Tower, P.O. Box 36036,
Minneapolis, Minnesota 55435 USA. International copyrights reserved in all countries.
No part of this book may be reproduced in any form without written permission from the
publisher.

Printed in the United States.

Cover and Interior Photo credits: Peter Arnold, Inc., SuperStock, Archive, Corbis-Bettmann

Edited by Lori Kinstad Pupeza
Contributing editor Brooke Henderson
Special thanks to our Checkerboard Kids—Peter Rengstorf, Stephanie McKenna,
Morgan Roberts

All statistics taken from the 1990 census; The Rand McNally Discovery Atlas of The
United States.

Library of Congress Cataloging-in-Publication Data

Joseph, Paul, 1970-
     Oklahoma / Paul Joseph.
     p. cm. -- (United States)
     Includes index.
     Summary: Surveys the people, geography, and history of the state known as the
"Sooner State."
     ISBN 1-56239-871-7
     1. Oklahoma--Juvenile literature. [1. Oklahoma.] I. Title. II. Series: United
States (Series)
     F694.3.J67 1998
     976.6--DC21
                                                97-18682
                                            CIP
                                            AC

Contents

Welcome to Oklahoma

The state of Oklahoma is unlike any other state. Its history is unusual. For many years the area was a **reservation** for Native Americans who were pushed off their own land. This land was given to the Native Americans by the United States.

The state remained untouched by white **settlers**. Settlers who were moving west would have to go around the state because they were not allowed to enter.

Later, white settlers tried to move into the state **illegally** and take the Native American's land. In 1889, the government officially opened Oklahoma to white settlers. The settlers moved in by the thousands and claimed land.

Oklahoma is nicknamed the "Sooner State." It is called this because many **settlers** moved into Oklahoma "sooner" than they should have.

This unusual history has inspired many books, plays, and movies. The play *Green Grow the Lilacs* was made into the musical comedy *Oklahoma!* This hit movie made the state a household word.

This wonderful state is known for its farming. However, the state is also filled with beautiful cities, excellent museums, big businesses, wonderful colleges, state parks, outdoor recreation, and great people.

A windmill and cattle tank in the Oklahoma panhandle.

Fast Facts

OKLAHOMA

Capital and Largest city
Oklahoma City (444,719 people)
Area
68,656 square miles
(177,818 sq km)
Population
3,157,604 people
Rank: 28th
Statehood
November 16, 1907
(46th state admitted)
Principal rivers
Arkansas River, Canadian River,
Red River
Highest point
Black Mesa;
4,973 feet (1,516 m)
Motto
Labor omnia vincit (Labor
conquers all things)
Song
"Oklahoma"
Famous People
Carl Albert, Woody Guthrie, Lynn
Riggs, Oral Roberts, Will Rogers,
Maria Tallchief, Jim Thorpe

*S*tate Flag

*M*istletoe

*S*cissor-tailed
Flycatcher

*R*edbud

About Oklahoma

The Sooner State

Detail area

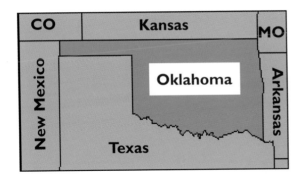

OK

Oklahoma's abbreviation

Borders: west (Texas, New Mexico), north (Kansas, Colorado), east (Missouri, Arkansas), south (Texas)

Nature's Treasures

Oklahoma's greatest natural treasures are its **minerals** and its rich soil. The mineral **petroleum** brings a lot of money to the state. Since the state's first major oil field was discovered near Tulsa in 1901, oil has been found in nearly all of Oklahoma's 77 counties.

Large oil fields also produce **natural gas**. Other minerals in the state are coal, zinc, lead, sand, gravel, stone, and clay.

Oklahoma's rich grazing land and warm climate are ideal for animals or livestock. The total number of farms is about 69,000.

Another treasure are the beautiful forests. In the eastern mountain regions of Oklahoma are millions of acres of forest. Wild animals are also a treasure in

Oklahoma. The Wichita Mountains Wildlife Refuge protects the buffalo, elk, deer, and longhorn **cattle** from hunters.

There are wonderful rivers and lakes in the Sooner State. This makes for great fishing, swimming, boating, and other water activities.

A winter wheat crop growing in front of an oil refinery.

Beginnings

The first person to explore in the area of Oklahoma was Francisco Coronado of Spain in the year 1541. He claimed the land for his home country. In 1682, Robert La Salle claimed the area for his own country of France.

More than 100 years later, in 1803, the United States purchased most of Oklahoma from France in what was known as the "**Louisiana Purchase**."

In 1830, the United States government passed the Indian Removal Act. This law said that Native Americans living in the southeastern part of the United States would be forced to move to Oklahoma.

This was a very sad time in American History. The Native Americans had to leave their land and most of their possessions to make the long move to Oklahoma. This was known as the Trail of Tears.

Five Native American tribes from southeastern areas—the Cherokee, Choctaw, Chickasaw, Creek, and Seminole—made Oklahoma home. They joined the Plains Indians that were already there. They began to prosper. They made farms and built schools.

However, on April 22, 1889, Oklahoma was opened to new white settlement. **Settlers** arrived on foot, horseback, wagon, and train to take land.

Together, the Native Americans and white settlers worked to be a part of the Union. On November 16, 1907, Oklahoma became part of the United States as the 46th state.

The Trail of Tears

B.C. to 1682

Early People of Oklahoma

Millions of years ago, dinosaurs roamed the area now known as Oklahoma.

The first known people to live in Oklahoma were the Plains Indians. These Native Americans were called the Caddo, Wichita, Pawnee, Osage, Cheyenne, and Arapaho.

1541: The first explorer from Europe to walk through Oklahoma is Francisco Coronado. He claims the area for Spain.

1682: Robert La Salle claims Oklahoma for France as part of French Louisiana.

Oklahoma

B.C. to 1682

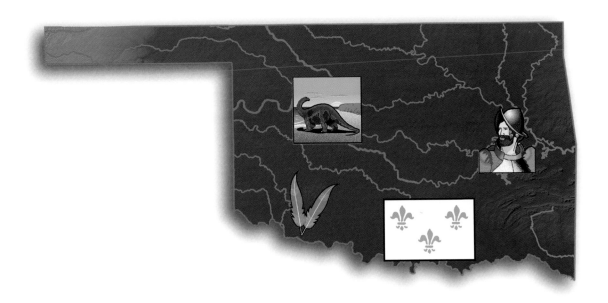

1803 to 1907

New Owners to Statehood

1803: The United States purchases the Louisiana region from France, which includes Oklahoma. This was called the **Louisiana Purchase**.

1830: The United States government passes the Indian Removal Act, which moves most Native Americans from southeastern United States to Oklahoma.

1889: Oklahoma's first oil well is drilled.

1889: On April 22 the government opens up Oklahoma to white **settlers**. This was one of the biggest land rushes in United States history.

1907: Oklahoma becomes the 46th state on November 16. Guthrie is chosen as the capital.

Oklahoma

1803 to 1907

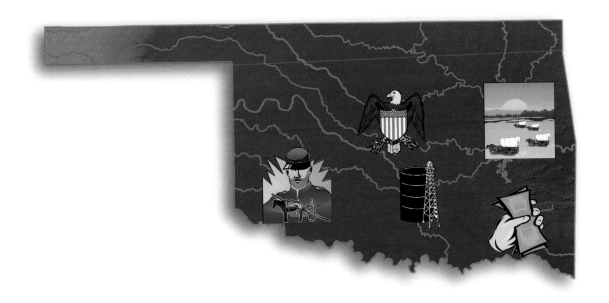

1910 to Now

Present Day Oklahoma
1910: The capital is moved to Oklahoma City.

1930s: Much of Oklahoma's wheat and cotton **crops** are ruined by severe **drought**. Many farmers leave their homes to find work in California.

1940: The Denison Dam is completed on the Red River. This forms Lake Texoma in 1943.

1978: A bad drought causes farmers to lose crops. The government gives Oklahoma money to help them.

1995: The worst **terrorist act** in United States history kills 168 people when a bomb blasts through the Oklahoma City Federal Building.

Oklahoma

1910 to Now

Oklahoma City

Oklahoma's People

There are just over three million people living in Oklahoma. It is the 28th most **populated** state in the nation.

Many famous people have come from Oklahoma. Baseball great Johnny Bench was born in Oklahoma City. He joined the Cincinnati Reds in 1967 and was National League Rookie of the Year in 1968. After winning two World Series titles and two Most Valuable Player Awards, he retired in 1983. Bench, one of the greatest catchers to play baseball, was elected to the Baseball Hall of Fame in 1989.

Author S.E. Hinton was born in Tulsa. In 1967, while she was still in high school, Hinton published her first book, *The Outsiders*. The popular book won many awards and later was made into a hit movie. Other books she wrote were *Rumble Fish, Tex,* and *That Was Then, This Is Now.*

In 1925, Maria Tallchief was born in Fairfax, Oklahoma. A daughter of an Osage Native American, she lived on a **reservation** during part of her childhood. She first danced in Russia, then for the New York City Ballet. She won awards for her dancing. In 1980 she started the Chicago City Ballet.

Maria Tallchief

Johnny Bench

Splendid Cities

Since the development of the oil **industry**, Oklahoma has turned from small towns to large cities with skyscrapers.

Oklahoma City is the capital and the largest city in Oklahoma. It is in the center of the state. The city is known for its **petroleum** products and meat-packing. It is also noted for being a lively city with many things to do.

Since April 19, 1995, Oklahoma City saw the worst **terrorist act** in United States history. A bomb blasted apart a Federal Building and killed 168 people. This also showed the world how the wonderful people of Oklahoma came together to help the victims and the victims' families.

20

In the northeast part of the state is the second largest city, Tulsa. This city is sometimes called the "oil capital of the world" because of all the oil fields around the city. Tulsa is filled with museums, parks, and a zoo. This fine city is also home to the University of Tulsa and Oral Roberts University.

Other splendid cities are Lawton, Broken Arrow, Edmond, Midwest City, Enid, Moore, and Stillwater.

Tulsa skyline over the Arkansas River.

Oklahoma's Land

Oklahoma is mostly a flat state. The land rises slowly from east to west to form mountains. There are also forests, lakes, and rivers. Oklahoma is divided into five distinct regions.

The Gulf Coastal Plain sits along the southeastern part of the state. This area has very fertile lowlands. Near the Arkansas **border** the Little River reaches the lowest point in Oklahoma at only 287 feet (87 m).

The Ouachita Mountains are in the far eastern part of the state. It is mainly covered with forest and mountains. The Ozark Plateau region is in the northeast. Here too,

Great Plains

Ozark Plateau

Central Plains

Ouachita Mountains

Gulf Coastal Plain

are forest and mountains. This area is also known for growing a lot of fruits and vegetables.

The Central Plains is the state's largest region. It covers most of the state except for the east and the Panhandle. This region is mainly rolling grassland. In the south-central part of this area are the Arbuckle Mountains. The Wichitas stand in the west.

The Great Plains cover the entire Panhandle. This area is covered with short buffalo grass. The trees in this region are found only along streams. In the far northwest corner is Black Mesa. This is a flat-topped hill that reaches 4,973 feet (1,516 m)—the highest point in the state.

A farm in the Great Plains

Oklahoma at Play

The people of Oklahoma and the many people who visit the state have a lot of places they can go.

In the mountains people can walk and hike. In the Wichita Mountains Wildlife Refuge people can see buffalo, elk, deer, and longhorn **cattle**.

In the many lakes people can fish, swim, or do other fun water sports. There are many wonderful parks and forests in Oklahoma.

Other fun activities include rodeos. Red Earth is one of the best festivals about Native American life in the country. It is held every year in Oklahoma City.

The city of Anadarko is a very popular attraction. It is the site of the American Indian Exposition, Indian City, U.S.A., the National Hall of Fame for American Indians, and the Southern Plains Indian Museum.

Oklahoma is full of beautiful parks and forests.

Oklahoma at Work

The people of Oklahoma must work to make money. A lot of people in the Sooner State work in **mining**. Within 60 miles (96 km) of Oklahoma City there are more than 5,000 oil wells! These oil wells provide many jobs and give nearly half of the state's total oil production.

Oklahoma has always been an important farming state. Farming provides many jobs for the Sooner State. The rich grazing land and excellent climate provide the best livestock raising.

Many people work on the 69,000 farms that are in the state. Farmers mostly grow winter wheat in Oklahoma. Other **crops** grown in the state include cotton, peanuts, pecans, hay, barley, soybeans, oats, and corn.

There are many different things to do in Oklahoma. Because of its beauty, people, land, mountains, forests, and history, the Sooner State is a great place to visit, live, work, and play.

A cotton farm in Oklahoma.

Fun Facts

• The city of Guthrie was the first capital of Oklahoma in 1890. It remained the capital when Oklahoma became a state in 1907. In 1910, it was moved to Oklahoma City, where it still is today.

• Thanks to the northern part of Texas, the state of Oklahoma is shaped like a pan. It even has a panhandle!

• Oklahoma is the 19th biggest state. Its land covers 68,656 square miles (177,818 sq km). However, in **population** it is only the 28th largest state.

• Many books and movies were set in Oklahoma. Two were classics that are still watched and read today. One was the musical, *Oklahoma!* The other was the classic novel, written by John Steinbeck, and later a classic film, *The Grapes of Wrath*.

A scene from the musical, Oklahoma!

Glossary

Border: neighboring states, countries, or waters.

Cattle: farm animals such as cows, bulls, and oxen.

Crops: the rows of plants that farmers grow, like corn, beans, or cotton.

Drought: not having any rain for a long time.

Illegal: not obeying the law.

Industry: many different types of businesses.

Louisiana Purchase: land that was bought by the United States government in 1803, which included part of Oklahoma.

Minerals: things found in the earth, such as rock, diamonds, or coal.

Miners: people who work underground to get minerals.

Mining: working underground to get minerals.

Natural Gas: a type of gas that is found in the earth's crust.

Petroleum: also known as oil. An oily liquid that is obtained from wells drilled in the ground. It is used to make gasoline, fuel oils, and other products.

Population: the number of people living in a certain place.

Reservation: land set aside for Native Americans.

Rural: outside of the city.

Settlers: people that move to a new land and build a community.

Terrorist act: a violent action done by a person, usually for political reasons.

Internet Sites

The Jeb Page
http://users.aol.com/LxWebb/JEB/MAINJEB.HTM
This is an amusing page with some fun sounds and cool links. Created by a rock band called Jeb.

Oklahoma Inter-Tribal Gallery
http://www.indart.com/gallery/gallery.htm
Here you will find fine art, in painting and sculpture, arts in clay, cultural items, beadwork and kachinas, with preview images of some of the finest works available anywhere. We also have historic and contemporary beadwork, pottery and artifacts.

These sites are subject to change. Go to your favorite search engine and type in Oklahoma for more sites.

PASS IT ON

Tell Others Something Special About Your State

To educate readers around the country, pass on interesting tips, places to see, history, and little unknown facts about the state you live in. We want to hear from you!

To get posted on ABDO & Daughters website, E-mail us at "mystate@abdopub.com"

Index

CLASSIC
SOURDOUGHS

CLASSIC
SOURDOUGHS

REVISED

A Home Baker's Handbook

ED WOOD AND JEAN WOOD

TEN SPEED PRESS

Berkeley

JEAN WOOD

October 21, 1928 – October 12, 2010

THIS BOOK IS dedicated to Jean, the coauthor of this book. We met on the campus of Oregon State University in 1948. In the decades since, she has been my companion in every aspect of my life—the soul of my aspirations.

We married in Boston on June 12, 1950. She brought us three sons and two daughters. As we raised our family, we also shared a lifetime of adventures. We especially loved the outdoors, catching salmon together along the West Coast, hunting for game birds throughout the United States and Canada, and enjoying camping and exploration.

She shared my obsession with sourdough breads and together we searched the Middle East and Europe for the sourdough culture that produced man's first leavened breads. Among ancient bakeries unearthed in Egypt, we discovered the culture that was used to feed the builders of the Giza pyramid.

Jean was loved by all who knew her. Her passion and conviction infuse the writing of this book. Shortly after its completion, she passed from us suddenly and without warning. In loving memory, I dedicate this book to her life and the vitality she brought to mine.

Published in the United States by Ten Speed Press, an imprint of the Crown Publishing Group,
a division of Random House, Inc., New York.
www.crownpublishing.com
www.tenspeed.com

Ten Speed Press and the Ten Speed Press colophon are registered trademarks of
Random House, Inc.

Originally published as *World Sourdoughs from Antiquity* by Sinclair Publishing, Cascade, ID,
in 1989. A revised edition was published by Ten Speed Press, Berkeley, in 1996, and reissued in
slightly different form as *Classic Sourdoughs: A Home Baker's Handbook* by Ten Speed Press,
Berkeley, in 2001.

Library of Congress Cataloging-in-Publication Data
Wood, Ed, 1926-
  Classic sourdoughs : a home baker's handbook / by Ed Wood and Jean Wood. — Rev. ed.
     p. cm.
  Includes index.
    Summary: "This authoritative sourdough baking classic is updated with a new technique
that allows the baker to control sourness and ensure consistently leavened loaves"
—Provided by publisher
  1. Cooking (Sourdough). 2. Sourdough bread. 3. Bread. 4. Cookbooks.
I. Wood, Jean, 1928-2010. II. Title.
  TX770.S66W66 2011
  641.8'15—dc22

                            2011009408

ISBN 978-1-60774-007-0

Printed in the United States of America on recycled paper (20% PCW)

Design by Chloe Rawlins
Front cover photograph © iStockphoto / Klaus Hollitzer

10 9

Revised Edition

CONTENTS

FIVE

Baking Sourdoughs with Bread Machines • 151

PREFACE

PEOPLE AROUND THE world are again becoming fascinated by sourdoughs. We see evidence of this interest daily here at Sourdoughs International, where we grow, harvest, and dry cultures that we have collected from around the world (see page 167 for descriptions of the cultures in our collection, and the stories behind them). Orders for these cultures come from places as disparate as South Africa, Japan, Australia, and Norway.

Why the fascination? The simple answer is that, in many ways, sourdoughs improve the quality of our lives. They have a unique, inherent charisma, and they still produce the best bread the world has ever known. They are soul-satisfying and fun: we call them "endorphins of the kitchen." They truly offer an extension of a personal quality beyond what we eat to what we do and what we are.

More than thirty years ago, we self-published *World Sourdoughs from Antiquity*. In 1996, it was revised and published by Ten Speed Press, which did a much better job with it than we did. In 2001, it was again revised and updated, this time under the title *Classic Sourdoughs: A Home Baker's Handbook*. Ten years later, this new edition keeps the heart of the previous editions and adds many refinements in technique and one important new method, the culture proof, which is designed to bring your refrigerated sourdough culture to vibrant life before you begin to bake, ensuring the best structure and flavor in the finished loaf.

This way of baking has enriched our lives tremendously. The purpose of this book is the same as it has been for the last three decades: to share with you the pleasures of using sourdoughs in your own kitchen.

INTRODUCTION

THIS BOOK WILL introduce you to the personal satisfaction and sense of accomplishment experienced by home bakers of traditional sourdough. If you are an experienced sourdough baker, it will guide you to the sourdoughs you seek.

Let's start by defining what we really mean by "traditional" sourdoughs. We know the sourdough process results from the fermentation reactions of two quite different classes of microorganisms: wild yeast and beneficial bacteria. For well over five thousand years, all breads were produced by the fermentation of these two essential microorganisms acting together. The yeasts are primarily responsible for leavening and bread texture, the bacteria for the sourdough flavor. Thus the definition of "traditional" sourdough requires a "culture," or "starter," containing both of these organisms.

Delicious, nutritious breads of various kinds were produced for centuries by a process no one understood. Bakers believed there was "something" in dough that made it rise. They knew if they saved some old dough and added it to a new batch, the new dough would also rise. For eons, all new doughs required a bit of old dough to "start" the rising process. In villages and towns around the world, bread was the staff of life—it literally supported life. People baked it in their homes, and every town had a bakery where the people could take their dough to be baked in the baker's oven, or buy bread from the baker himself. When people emigrated to the United States, they brought their dough starters with them. The California forty-niners and the Yukon and Alaskan miners get credit for the term "sourdoughs," probably due to the extreme flavor of their breads (the crusty miners themselves subsequently became known as "sourdoughs"). Thus our definition of "traditional" sourdough also requires a culture with organisms that, with proper care, will survive and replicate themselves forever.

In the 1800s, Louis Pasteur looked into a microscope and saw what we now call wild yeast, discovering for the first time what really made bread dough rise. Within the next hundred years, researchers learned how to select, isolate, and grow single strains of yeast in pure cultures. They searched for and found species of *Saccharomyces cerevisiae*, baker's yeast, which leavened bread doughs with incredible speed.

Then industry took bread out of the home and put it in factories that manufacture something labeled "bread," which neither looks nor tastes like the staff of life. Breads began to be produced by mammoth machines. Sourdough starters were no longer used, small-town bakeries disappeared, people stopped baking in their homes, and the staff of life became neither delicious nor nutritious. Bakers thought the need for sourdough cultures was gone forever, but they were wrong. Baker's yeast is totally incapable of producing sourdough flavor, and without the action of lactobacilli in concert with yeast, the quality of breads has never been the same—not even close.

Within just the last hundred years, there have been monumental changes to what we call bread, and these changes are mostly for the worse. Not only do huge baking machines now dominate the production of bread, the baking industry adds a plethora of chemicals to flour and dough to change their physical characteristics and improve their "machinability." These include surface-active agents (surfactants) to help doughs go through machinery without sticking or tearing, other chemicals to soften the final bread texture or strengthen the dough by modifying the gluten, and a host of emulsifiers just to improve the mixing characteristics or increase shelf life. All of these additives have one thing in common: no, or very limited, nutritional value. At least one of them, potassium bromate, has been banned worldwide as a potential carcinogen.

In centralized industrial bakeries, large baking conglomerates produce packaged breads and refrigerated or frozen dough for distribution to retail stores and local bakeries. The distribution of industrial bread doughs means that even if a bread is baked fresh at a local bakery, it often still contains all the additives and chemicals included by the wholesale producers to grease its progress through the massive machinery—and none of the beneficial microflora that make bread taste like bread. And this is not only an American story: the deterioration of bread quality is a worldwide phenomenon, occurring even in the European heartlands of great bread.

In spite of these monumental changes, a small cadre of hardy souls have continued using the old-fashioned sourdough methods and today they are widely celebrated as "artisan" bakers. They have persisted in baking traditional sourdoughs, and in the past few decades, the market for their products has blossomed. Industrial bread still lumbers on, dominating the market, but it is easier now than it has been in many years to find real, old-fashioned sourdough breads—or to make them at home.

The best breads available today are being produced in the home or in artisan bakeries. But in our kitchens, the techniques are not the same as those used by the artisan bakers, or by the pioneers. Early home bakers used their starters to bake almost every day. Most of us now start with a culture that has become dormant between uses. The production capacity of the artisan baker requires masonry or special ovens and equipment beyond the scope of the individual home baker. For that reason, this book is designed specifically for and dedicated to the individual who bakes for him or herself or for a family and who deserves the thrill and joy of traditional sourdoughs.

ONE

The Birth and Life of Sourdough

IT TOOK UNCOUNTED centuries for wheat and other grains used for flour to evolve. Jarmo, in the uplands of Iraq, is one of the oldest archaeological excavations in the Middle East, dating to about 8000 BC. Here, archaeologists have identified carbonized kernels and clay imprints of plants that resemble wild and domesticated wheats. Historians believe that similar grains were established in Egypt by at least the same time, and perhaps as early as 10,000 to 15,000 BC. Rye existed in the Middle East as an unwanted weed and eventually spread across the Mediterranean to the Baltic countries, where it dominates bread making to this day. These wild grasses took millennia to progress to grain-producing plants, and it was many centuries before humans learned to cultivate and use them for food.

Grains like wheat and rye were probably first consumed as porridge. Eventually, this gruel evolved into a flat cake of baked cereal—baked perhaps on a hot rock in the fire. But how did these flat, hard cakes rise for the first time and become bread? An unbaked cake, perhaps forgotten on a warm summer evening, would be a perfect medium for contamination by an errant wild yeast. Imagine how many times that accident occurred before someone saw it and then baked it! It must have taken a thousand years, a thousand accidents, and finally a thousand experiments to produce a recognizable loaf of bread.

The Discovery of Yeast

In 1676, a Dutch lens grinder, Anton van Leeuwenhoek, first observed and described microscopic life, and in 1680, he produced the first sketches of yeast in beer. But for the next 170 years, nothing more happened to further our understanding of bread's secrets. Then in 1857, Louis Pasteur proved that fermentation is caused by yeast, and a comprehensive system of yeast classification, which we still use, was published in 1896.

With Pasteur's work, a whole new field of yeast technology and cereal chemistry came to life. Microbiologists learned how to isolate single yeast cells and to select pure cultures. They selectively bred wild strains to develop yeast cells that leavened faster, were more tolerant to temperature change, and were easier to produce commercially. Modern mass-produced cakes of pressed yeast and packages of active dried yeast contain billions of cells that are all exactly alike. These purified strains are carefully guarded to prevent contamination by wild types.

Cereal chemists were at work, too, learning to control the texture and appearance of bread by bleaching and blending different types of flour. They found a host of chemical additives to improve the consistency of dough and change its flavor, and to increase the shelf life of the finished loaf and improve its nutritional value. Agronomists selected for and bred wheat varieties that resist disease, produce bigger yields per acre, contain more protein, and so on. These advances all contributed to the industrial production of bread, with huge machines producing thousands of loaves per day. Now a handful of very large bakeries produce more than three-fourths of all bread sold in the United States. These same "advances" have also resulted in the fact that most modern bread has the flavor of an edible napkin.

Yeasts are microfungi and are much larger than most bacteria. More than 350 different species exist, with countless additional strains and varieties. In the century and a half since Louis Pasteur discovered that yeast fermentation produces carbon dioxide, which leavens dough, yeasts have been studied in every conceivable light and harnessed to perform hundreds of different tasks, from cleaning up oil slicks to producing antibiotics. Many yeast strains are industrially produced for very specific functions, including commercial bread making.

It is important to understand the basic differences between the wild yeasts of sourdough and the commercial baker's yeast used in most other breads. First, sourdough yeasts grow best in acidic doughs, while baker's yeast does better in neutral or slightly alkaline doughs. Baker's yeast is a single species, *Saccharomyces cerevisiae*, with hundreds of strains and varieties, while sourdoughs are usually leavened by one or more species in the same dough, none of them baker's yeast. Baker's yeast is a highly uniform product that produces an equally uniform texture in bread dough. The wild yeasts are anything but uniform, and they vary from region to region. But perhaps the most impressive difference between the two yeast types is that a single package of instant dried yeast produces just one batch of bread, while the same amount of wild sourdough culture produces loaf after loaf for the lifetimes of many bakers.

In one gram of commercial cake yeast, there are 20 to 24 billion individual yeast cells; in a package of dry yeast, there are 130 billion. By comparison, a cup of sourdough culture as it comes from the refrigerator contains far fewer cells. This book emphasizes repeatedly that you should never use baker's yeast either in your sourdough culture or in the recipe of your sourdough bread. The addition of baker's yeast to a culture may overwhelm the wild yeast and destroy the culture. In addition, you risk the introduction of a bacteriophage, or virus, to which the commercial cells are immune but which may kill wild yeast. Plus, if you leaven your dough with baker's yeast, the open texture characteristic of sourdough may disappear.

The primary secret of sourdough success lies in the art of stimulating a wild culture, just before you use it in baking, into a burst of activity to equal the number of yeast cells found in commercial yeast. The steps we describe to prepare and proof a culture in this book lead to that burst of activity and ensure you will get all the leavening power your loaf needs without the addition of commercial yeast.

Research into Wild Sourdough Cultures

Bakers of every sort welcomed the introduction of commercial yeast in the late 1800s. It greatly simplified the baking process and made it much faster. But something happened to the sourdough flavor. It disappeared! In due time, researchers identified the problem. They found that sourdough bread is the product of not one microorganism but two: wild yeasts make it rise and beneficial bacteria provide the flavor. These bacteria are primarily lactobacilli, so named because they produce lactic acid, which contributes to the sour flavor. But what lactobacilli do, they don't do very fast. It requires approximately twelve hours for the bacteria to develop fully the authentic taste of sourdough, depending on the temperature of the dough. Extremely fast commercial yeasts, particularly active dry yeast, have shortened the rising process to two hours or less, hardly giving the lactobacilli a chance to get started.

Lactobacilli produce the flavor of sourdough breads by fermentation, which is the primary reason sourdoughs are completely different from, and better than, most commercial breads. Fermentation is that process by which a variety of bacterial organisms act on food products to produce different flavors, textures, and aromas. Examples include the fermentation of milk to produce cheese, yogurt, sour cream, and buttermilk. Many types of sausage involve fermentation of various meats. Fermentation is also essential in the production of various vegetable preparations, including pickles, sauerkraut, olives, and a host of dishes from every corner of the earth. Finally, of course, wine and beer are made through the process of fermentation. But few of us are aware that fermentation is essential to the flavor of sourdoughs. Without sufficient time for that process to occur, the flavor will be lost.

Lactobacilli that produce the famous taste of San Francisco sourdough have been studied by Leo Kline and T. F. Sugihara, two food scientists working at the Western Regional Laboratory of the Department of Agriculture in Albany, California. They determined that many bakeries in the area were using sourdough colonized by identical strains of yeast and lactobacilli. The widespread occurrence of these organisms was not because the bakeries shared their starters with one another, but because these organisms are dominant throughout the San Francisco area. This led them to name this strain of bacteria *Lactobacillus sanfrancisco*. In 1970 and 1971, they published the results of their studies on San Francisco sourdough in *The Bakers Digest* and *Applied Microbiology*.

Kline and Sugihara identified for the first time the wild yeast *Torulopsis holmii* (later reclassified as *Candida milleri*, now as *Candida humilis*) as the wild yeast responsible for the sourdough process and provided instructions for producing it. The yeast also has an unusual characteristic: it is unable to utilize maltose, one of the carbohydrates found in flour. This assumes special significance, since the lactobacilli require the maltose unused by the yeast. Thus a symbiosis arises between the two organisms in the medium of hydrated flour. Further evidence indicates that the lactobacilli produce an antibiotic that protects the culture from contamination by harmful bacteria. This strong mutual dependence is thought to be responsible for the survival of the culture in San Francisco bakeries for more than one hundred years. It also explains why the culture successfully resists contamination when used in other areas. In 1973, Kline and Sugihara applied for and received a patent based on those studies so that, in the words of the patent, "the unique product (San Francisco sourdough) can be manufactured efficiently, economically and in any location regardless of climate or topography."

The work of Kline and Sugihara was intended for use by commercial bakers, but with modifications it is extremely helpful to home bakers as well. When the research was being done, San Francisco bakers "rebuilt" the starter every eight hours, several days a week (we'll note that current methods suggest that this timing was more an accommodation to the eight-hour workday than to the needs of the culture). When starters were rebuilt, 25 to 40 percent of the previous starter was used to rebuild the new one. This provided a massive inoculum of the microorganisms and a very acidic environment from the very beginning, which helped prevent contamination by other organisms. When the starter was used in a bread recipe, however, it represented only 11 percent of the total mix, while many artisan bakeries today use as much as 40 percent. The starter sponge was made with high-gluten flour milled from Montana spring wheat containing 14 percent protein, while the recipe used a regular "patent" flour. Artisan bakers now often use all-purpose flour for both. After mixing, the starter was proofed for seven to eight hours at 75° to 80°F (24° to 27°C). Once the loaves were formed, they received an additional proofing of six to eight hours at 85° to 90°F (29° to 32°C). Artisan and home bakers now commonly proof longer at room temperature. It must be emphasized that Kline and Sugihara used a specific sourdough culture with the organisms they identified and that, until 1998, artisan and home bakers were usually not able to acquire that culture.

Additional studies have looked at sourdoughs from Italy, the Middle East, India, Denmark, and Germany. Unlike most bacteria, lactobacilli thrive in the acid environment of sourdough and produce a variety of mild organic acids, alcohols, and many additional compounds vital to the flavor of the doughs. One researcher has listed no fewer than fifty-five separate compounds in sourdoughs—many of them, of course, present only in trace amounts.

Research on bacteria that ferment bread is minuscule compared to the work on milk, meat, and vegetable fermentations. Although much of the research on other foods is not directly related to sourdoughs, many analogies are valuable in understanding the action of bacteria in bread doughs. Work on milk fermentation has identified a group of factors that inhibit the growth of starter bacteria in the production of cheese and yogurt. These include antibiotics present in the milk of cows that have been treated to prevent udder infections and in sanitizers used in cleaning milking machines. These findings point out the importance of never adding anything to your sourdough culture except flour and water. Further, if you experience inconsistent results with recipes calling for milk, inhibitors of this type may be involved.

Sourdough research in Germany and Denmark has also revealed the presence of different lactobacilli. Sourdough cultures appear to be colonized by the specific types of yeast and lactobacilli found where the cultures originate, which explains why breads from different areas often have distinctive characteristics. While directing the pathology department of a hospital laboratory in Saudi Arabia, Ed studied the microbiology of sourdough cultures we collected during our travels in the Middle East and Europe. Each contained a dominant yeast accompanied by several strains of lactobacilli. The wild yeast in each of the cultures revealed different physical characteristics under the microscope. We isolated both yeasts and bacteria in pure culture, then recombined them to test the combination after excluding interfering organisms. Detailed studies demonstrated that each culture represented a different yeast-lactobacillus combination, consisting of one wild yeast and two to four different lactobacillus strains.

Our studies moved from the laboratory to home kitchens, where thirty of our friends and associates tested the baking and taste differences. They helped to confirm that, indeed, each culture, whether it was from Bahrain or Saudi Arabia or San Francisco, produced a different bread.

We wondered, could one of those cultures be the same combination that puzzled the first baker ten thousand years before? We felt, at times, close to that ancient person who first saw sourdough bubbles.

The Rebirth of an Ancient Sourdough Culture

In early March, 1993, our phone rang. It was an editor with the National Geographic Society asking if we would like to help Dr. Mark Lehner, an Egyptologist for the Oriental Institute of the University of Chicago, and a team from the magazine rediscover how the Egyptians baked man's first leavened bread 5,000 years ago to feed the pyramid builders. Needless to say, we said we would like that very much.

The Society sent us to the Giza area and the adventure began. There was some doubt that the Egyptian authorities would permit us to conduct our experiments in the ancient bakery that Mark had discovered, or even have access to the baking vessels and tools he had recovered. As an alternative, Mark proposed that we build a replica somewhere in the desert near the pyramids and have the baking dishes and molds reproduced by a local pottery maker, so this is what we did.

Archaeologists have noted the increased occurrence of new grains in the era when the pyramids were built. We now recognize these as the ancestors of modern wheat. All of the wheats belong to the genus *Triticum,* and evolved from various wild grasses. One of the first to develop was emmer, *T. dicoccum* (its species name indicates that each husk covers two seeds). Emmer has good gluten content and the Egyptians used it to bake leavened bread, but the husks cling tightly to the grain and are difficult to remove. So when later grains appeared with husks that literally fell off during threshing—the so-called "naked" wheats—they quickly became favored over emmer. (However, in upper Egypt between Assiut and Aswan, an ancient wheat is still being grown in very small parcels for personal use. Its name is *T. pyramidal*—that name does have a ring to it.)

While Mark was completing the replica of the ancient bakery, we made a trip to the tomb of Teti, located just south of Sakkara, the city of the dead. Among the pictures on the tomb walls are men with offerings to the king of great loaves of cone-shaped bread balanced on each shoulder. It was an illustration of what we were supposed to produce. But first we had to capture and activate a culture.

We were sure we could find a sourdough culture in Giza, hopefully a descendant of one that had been leavening bread along the Nile for five thousand years. But if we used flour from the United States that was already contaminated with wild yeast or bacteria, when we tried to catch a culture at Giza, we would not know which organisms were actually present. So we arranged with friends at the Mountain States Tumor Institute in Idaho to try to sterilize Kamut (a "naked" wheat that is nevertheless a close relative of emmer) using ionizing radiation. Their efforts succeeded, and we were able to take to Egypt a quantity of Kamut flour that was sterile and whose gluten was completely undamaged.

Just five days after exposing our sterile Kamut (mixed with the right amount of water) at the foot of a pyramid, we captured a fabulous Giza culture from antiquity. In the next five days, in the replica of the open ancient bakery, Jean kneaded a great quantity of loaves and Ed baked sourdoughs over coal in domed bread pots like those the ancient Egyptians used (we call them the world's first home baking machines). The large cone-shaped loaves looked just like ancient leavened bread as depicted on the tomb walls, and the project was proclaimed a success by an enthusiastic National Geographic team. The flavor of these loaves was typical of authentic sourdough.

We took that fabulous culture home, and wondered if a single ancient culture captured during those five days at the foot of an Egyptian pyramid would play a role in the rebirth of sourdoughs. After *National Geographic* magazine released the story of our adventure, in January, 1995, we knew it would.

TWO

The Ingredients of Sourdough Bread

A GOOD CONSISTENT culture (starter) is one of the more essential ingredients for sourdough success. Wild cultures are a mixture of several strains of wild yeast and lactobacilli. The foam on top of a culture is evidence of wild yeast activity for leavening, but it is not a good indicator of the growth of lactobacilli, which are needed for sourness and flavor. There are a multitude of methods suggested to ensure the presence of this bacterial component, most of them worthless. Yogurt has been recommended as a source of the lactobacilli, but yogurt bacteria metabolize the proteins of milk, not the starches of grain, so a stable synergistic culture is not likely to develop—and it may be necessary to add milk to the culture as a nutrient. Furthermore, milk may contain antibiotics used to treat udder disease in cows or trace amounts of disinfectants used to sterilize milking equipment, either of which may destroy the organisms of a sourdough culture. Other methods include using grapes, apples, or potato water. All of these may have airborne lactobacilli on their surfaces, but these are the same organisms that are better collected directly from the air. When you use a flour and water mixture to collect a culture, the lactobacilli that grow are those that are capable of utilizing the starches of flour; these are more likely to form a symbiosis with wild yeast to produce a culture with long-term stability.

Your Sourdough Culture

Your culture will last your lifetime with proper care. The organisms you collect may be descendants of those a hundred or a thousand years old and the culture cannot be easily destroyed except by too much heat. Never expose it to temperatures above 100°F (38°C).

It should be stored in the refrigerator, but do not freeze it, as some wild yeasts may not survive. You can refrigerate your culture for six months without feeding it, but it is easier to maintain if it is fed every two to four months. If you do not plan to bake, and the culture has been in the refrigerator for about four months, it is a good idea to feed and warm it until it is fully active and then refrigerate it again.

Never add baker's yeast to it and do not use baker's yeast in a sourdough bread recipe. Ironically, commercial bakers have just the opposite concern: they take measures to prevent the contamination of their cultures with wild yeast.

Do not add anything but flour and water to your culture. The effect on wild yeast of leftovers from bread dough, salt, sugar, spices, and other ingredients is unpredictable and therefore undesirable. Avoid contamination of the culture with chemicals.

Many home bakers use more than one sourdough culture and worry that one may contaminate and displace the organisms of the others. In general, we don't believe this to be a significant problem. Stable cultures are characterized by organisms that have become dominant over extremely long periods of time, with symbiotic relationships that are difficult to disrupt. However, one should use some precautions to prevent gross contamination: we do not bake with different cultures at the same time.

When a culture is stored in the refrigerator, the yeast organisms become dormant. After extended refrigeration, some of the yeast cells and bacteria will be damaged and die. It is desirable to have a high concentration of active yeast at the start of cooling to produce a maximum number of cells that will regenerate the culture when it is warmed. Before putting your culture back in the refrigerator after taking some out for baking, you should feed it ²/₃ cup (90 g) of flour and enough water to maintain a thick pancake-batter consistency, and proof for an hour or two at 85°F (29°C).

During refrigeration, it is normal for a brownish liquid to form on top of the culture. This is a mixture of organic alcohols formed during fermentation and has no adverse effect. Just mix it into the culture before using.

Sourdoughs International offers a choice of cultures collected from around the world. These cultures are dried at low temperatures to preserve the viability of the organisms. Properly dried, cultures are amazingly stable as long as they are not exposed to excessive heat. We have received many reports of misplaced dried cultures that are discovered in refrigerators or odd storage places after three to four years that have been successfully activated and used. Cultures are activated simply by adding flour and water and proofing. Once activated, they should be refrigerated, not frozen.

There is a well-known myth that moving a culture from one location to another will result in its becoming contaminated by the local organisms. That is absolute nonsense without an iota of evidence. Usually what really happens is that the baker fails to take proper care of the culture and blames the culture when it fails to perform well.

Capturing Your Own Culture

It is entirely feasible to capture your own culture by simply exposing a mixture of flour and water to the air. When the right organisms find your mixture, they will grow and thrive. Usually the wrong ones won't even survive on flour and water. Since authentic sourdough recipes often call for only flour, water, and salt, don't try to collect a culture on grapes, potatoes, or other esoteric substances. If there is growth of organisms that use these nutrients, it will not be authentic sourdough.

So, mix 2 cups (280 g) of flour and 1½ cups (380 ml) of warm water in a 2-quart (2 liter) plastic or glass bowl. Stir the mixture with sufficient vigor to beat in additional air. Expose the bowl and its contents to the air, preferably outside, though it can be done inside as well. Do not cover the bowl with plastic or anything else that will exclude the organisms you are attempting to collect. If insects or other critters are a potential problem, the bowl should be covered with a fine mesh screen or cheesecloth. Stir the mixture vigorously at least twice every twenty-four hours. In two or three days, some bubbles should appear on the surface as the first indication of success. At this point, feed it an additional cup (140 g) of flour and sufficient water to maintain the consistency and stir it briskly again. You may need to repeat additional feedings at twelve- to twenty-four-hour intervals for several successive days. When you capture a yeast that is active enough to be useful, it will form a layer of foam 1 to 2 inches (2.5 to 5 cm) deep. If it doesn't attain this level of activity in four to five days, you should probably abandon the attempt and repeat the process in a different location. There is no guarantee that you'll collect good lactobacilli, and you may encounter problems with contamination by undesirable organisms that also use flour as a nutrient. These organisms usually produce a bad odor.

Once you have a good, bubbly culture, transfer it to one or more quart (liter) glass jars and refrigerate. It may now be ready for use, but only successful baking will prove its worth. Don't freeze it, as some strains of wild yeast won't survive freezing. Don't leave it on the kitchen counter for several days without feeding it, or the activity of the lactobacilli will make the mixture too acidic and inhibit the yeast.

Wheat Flours

Plant geneticists have produced a large number of wheat varieties designed for highly specific conditions and requirements, taking into account soil type, growing temperatures, average rainfall, protein content, disease resistance, harvesting characteristics, yields per acre, and even adaptability to automated bread making machines. These varieties fall into four major categories: hard and soft winter wheat, and hard and soft spring wheat. Hard wheat has "strong" gluten, which some believe is required to trap the leavening gases and to form and maintain the shape of the bread loaf. Soft wheat has "weaker" gluten and is used to make various pastries, crackers, and similar products.

Spring wheat is planted in the spring and harvested in late summer. In North America, it is grown primarily in Montana, the Dakotas, Minnesota, and Canada, since the winters are often too cold for the wheat to survive if planted in the fall. This wheat is known throughout the world as Manitoba or Dark Northern Spring, and it is considered to be the wheat with the strongest gluten. Winter wheat is planted in the fall, lies dormant over winter, and is harvested in early summer.

An additional variable is the method of milling, which is the grinding and sifting process that produces flour from grain kernels. During milling, the kernel components are separated, depending on the type of flour being produced. The largest portion is the endosperm, which contains about 75 percent of the kernel's protein and is the sole source of white flour. Bran is the outer coating of the kernel, and it is included in whole wheat flour. The embryo or sprouting section of the seed is the germ. It contains fats and oils and is usually separated from flours, since it leads to rancidity during storage at room temperature.

In ancient times, milling was done by hand between two heavy stones, which not only removed the kernel's husk but ground the remaining portions so finely that they could not be separated. Some modern milling techniques still utilize special millstones, but millers who use them can now regulate the degree of fineness and separate the kernel components. Some believe, however, that stone milling is done primarily for its image and promotional value: these flours are highly touted to the home baker. High-speed steel roller milling remains the most common method, and the choice is largely one of personal preference. The type of wheat is far more important to the sourdough baker than the milling process.

White flour is available in two major categories. Bleached flours are treated with chlorine compounds or other bleaching agents to whiten the flour and may also have a number of chemical additives to improve baking characteristics. We believe that bleach and other additives may not be suitable for use with sourdough organisms. Unbleached flours generally have no chemical additives. Both bleached and unbleached white flours are usually enriched with iron and several of the B vitamins.

Lower gluten flours are often treated with oxidizing agents to strengthen their gluten. They may be blended with several other flour types, and may even include barley. Unfortunately, labels on flour rarely list the types of wheat they contain. In fact, most flours are a mixture of types, but the proportions and types remain a mystery. All-purpose flours are in this group of mixed-type flours. Because sourdough bakers want a unique, open texture and don't like a variety of chemicals, we prefer unbleached all-purpose flours. High-gluten flours produce the even texture desired by commercial bread bakers—this quality is not highly desirable for sourdough bakers.

One particular caution justifies a special paragraph. Avoid self-rising or instant flours, which may contain dried yeast or chemical leavens or both. In general, 1 cup (140 g) of self-rising flour contains $1^1/_2$ teaspoons of leavening agent and $^1/_2$ teaspoon of salt.

Grinding your own whole wheat is one way—perhaps the best way—to guarantee the type and quality of your flour and may offer a source of satisfaction worth the effort. Whole wheat flours contain most of the wheat kernel components and are more nutritious than white flours. However, enrichment standards established by the FDA in the early 1940s for white flours have lessened the nutritional differences between the two types. Whole wheat generally contains part or all of the wheat germ and will become rancid unless stored in the refrigerator or freezer. Cracked wheat is cut rather than ground and is used in bread recipes for special texture and flavor. Flaked and rolled wheat is also available.

Organic wheat flours are becoming more widely available in bulk food sections and health food stores. If organic foods are important to you for health or even moral reasons, you can bake organic sourdough breads more cheaply than you can buy them.

After many experiments, we have become convinced that "better for bread" flour with its "stronger" gluten is not necessarily better for sourdough bread. Strong gluten resists stretching and forms small, uniform holes, producing an uninteresting texture. The preferred sourdough texture, or "crumb," has large, irregular holes. We now use unbleached all-purpose flour, with its somewhat weaker gluten (unfortunately, many all-purpose flours are blended with flours of hard wheat and closely resemble bread flours). The recipes in this book specify unbleached all-purpose flour, but the choice is yours.

Kamut Flour

Kamut has an intriguing history shrouded in controversy. It starts some sixty years ago when a military serviceman stationed in Portugal was given a few grains of wheat said to be from King Tut's tomb. This "King Tut's grain" found its way to the Quinn ranch in Montana, where it was planted and produced organically for a number of years. In the 1980s, Bob Quinn studied the grain, classified it as *Triticum polonicum,* and labeled it Kamut, an Egyptian word for wheat. It has since been identified as khorasan wheat, a subspecies of *Triticum turgidum* and a close relation of emmer, the great-grandfather of modern wheat. Unlike emmer, Kamut is a so-called "naked" wheat—one that threshes free of its hull—as are all modern wheats. Quinn has trademarked the grain and continues to produce it organically on his Montana ranch and licenses it to be grown and marketed around the world: in a recent conversation with Quinn, he told me he sells more Kamut in Italy than anywhere else, including the United States. It is widely available in natural groceries and health food stores. It imparts a distinctive nutty flavor in sourdough bread.

Spelt Flour

Spelt may be even more ancient than Kamut and is said by some to have emerged more than nine thousand years ago. It has been popular in Europe for thousands of years and is currently common in European food stores. Our sourdough culture from Australia was collected on spelt.

Spelt, like emmer, has a tough husk that is difficult to remove, requiring special dehusking equipment. It was introduced to this country by Amish farmers in Ohio, who fed it primarily to livestock. In the 1980s, Wilhelm Kosnopfl, president of Michigan-based Purity Foods, financed a spelt research program at Ohio University and subsequently developed a facility at Okemos, Michigan, to provide spelt products to health food stores. I had an opportunity to have a brief chat with Willy Kosnopfl early in 1996, during which he remarked that "in Europe, spelt is used almost exclusively with sourdoughs." We both speculated that there may be something intrinsic about sourdough fermentations that is particularly well adapted to spelt flours. Indeed, spelt is a remarkable grain that produces terrific sourdough breads. The flour yields a soft, satiny dough with minimal kneading, and has a mild, pleasant taste.

The original marketing of spelt was a bit flamboyant, describing it as a "non-wheat" grain and therefore ideal for gluten-sensitive individuals. However, most agronomists consider spelt as a distinct species of wheat. Those with wheat allergies should use it with caution.

Don Stinchcomb, now the president of Purity Foods, says that health food fans appreciate spelt's unique nutritional qualities. According to Stinchcomb, spelt is higher in B vitamins and fiber than ordinary bread wheats and has larger amounts of both simple and complex carbohydrates. Studies by a number of researchers seem to indicate that spelt's gluten degrades rapidly during mixing, suggesting that mixing times should be limited for best results.

Most of our test baking for this book was with sourdough cultures grown in a mixture of all-purpose flour and water. When testing spelt flours, however, we used a culture with a spelt-water mixture so that we could evaluate doughs containing 100 percent spelt. The results were impressive. The culture itself had an entirely different texture than an all-purpose flour culture, almost like thick whipped cream. We baked recipes with 100 percent white spelt flour and with mixtures of whole spelt flour up to 68 percent. The loaves uniformly leavened as well as doughs of the same recipe using 100 percent all-purpose flour. We compared kneading for five minutes and ten minutes and could detect no difference.

The product we evaluated is Vita-Spelt, produced by Purity Foods. It is advertised as organic, unenriched, unbleached, and unbromated, which in the current era is impressive. The breads we baked were exquisite sourdoughs, and we have included several recipes for you to try. The flour at this time is a little pricey, but we think you'll find it worth the extra cost.

If your objective is to avoid "nonspelt glutens" and bake breads made entirely with spelt, transfer your culture from a bread flour base to a spelt flour base. This is quite easy to do. If you are activating a dried culture, simply substitute white spelt flour for white bread flour. If you have an activated bread flour culture, put $^1/_4$ cup (60 ml) into a 1-quart (1 liter) Mason jar, add 1 cup (240 ml) of warm water, stir vigorously, and add 1 cup (130 g) of white spelt flour. Stir briefly and proof at 85°F (29°C) for approximately twelve hours. Then take $^1/_4$ cup (60 ml) of this culture and repeat the process. After three or four repetitions, you will have diluted the bread flour to an insignificant level.

Durum Flour

At one time, we thought durum was a soft wheat used almost exclusively to produce pastas, such as macaroni, spaghetti, ravioli, noodles, and so on. All the soft stuff was made, we assumed, from "soft" wheat called durum. And then there's semolina, a coarse durum used to sprinkle on baking sheets or stones to keep dough from sticking. But we never heard of anyone using durum to bake bread until a decade or so ago, when we learned about it from North Dakota farmer Arlen Gilbertson, who grows it and is proud of his crop. He would hold a grain between his fingers and point out that it was almost transparent—then he'd tap it with a hammer to demonstrate its hardness. Durum is a spring wheat, and when Gilbertson told us that the protein content was between 14 and 17 percent, we began to get interested. Did that high protein mean high gluten? We wondered why no one was making bread with it. (We've since learned that it is widely used for bread baking in the Middle East.)

Our first baking trials were disappointing. At a level of 25 percent durum, there was a definite reduction in leavening. But the flavor was exceptionally good. We couldn't understand why what we now knew was a hard wheat with a high percentage of protein wouldn't have good gluten. But not all glutens are alike; further, there seems to be no direct relationship between gluten quality and percent protein. That is, a high protein is not always associated with high gluten and a low protein may have high gluten. Durum wheat and its glutens have been selected to produce certain qualities in pastas, but those glutens are not noted for their leavening qualities, as are other wheat glutens.

Rye Flour

In the United States, rye grain is grown mainly in the Dakotas, Minnesota, and Nebraska, in soils suitable for hardy grain varieties. It is a winter grain, planted in the fall and harvested the following summer. Rye protein is not of the gluten-forming type, and breads made entirely with rye flour do not rise well. It is usually mixed with wheat flour, producing a lighter loaf with rye flavor. Sourdough cultures originating in central Europe may be better adapted to fermenting rye, where it has been a dominant grain for centuries. These flours continue to be a major ingredient in the breads of many European countries.

When milling rye, two basic types of flour are produced: white and dark. White rye flour is made only from the endosperm. It is particularly recommended for mild-flavored Jewish and other light rye breads. It is generally mixed with 60 to 70 percent good-quality white flour. Dark rye is a more distinctive flavored flour especially suitable for heavy, dark rye breads such as German rye, Swedish rye, and pumpernickel. It is usually mixed with about 80 percent high-protein white or whole wheat flour. Pumpernickel flour is a coarse dark rye made by grinding the entire rye kernel. It is analogous to whole wheat and is milled in fine, medium, and coarse pumpernickel flours. Rye blends that combine regular or dark rye with a good-quality, high-protein white flour are also available.

Flax Flour

One of the subjects at a Canadian conference on nutrition we attended in 1998 was the benefits of the omega-3 fatty acids in flax. We acquired some samples of milled flax and whole flaxseed for bake tests with sourdough. All the loaves with varying percentages of flax flour leavened well and had an unusual whole grain flavor.

Health claims of one sort or another are made for flax and for other fibers, including durum and certain barleys. This is not necessarily the best reason to change your diet to include these fibers. However, they do add something special to the flavor and texture of sourdough breads, and they might increase your longevity. And one thing is certain: you can enjoy any benefits of omega-3 for a lot lower cost from flax than from salmon.

Bulgur Flour

Bulgur is not a special variety of wheat. Rather, it is almost any wheat prepared by a special method that was probably developed accidentally while in pursuit of long-term preservation. It is made by soaking and cooking the whole wheat kernel, drying it, and then removing part of the bran and cracking the remaining kernel into small pieces. Bulgur is man's oldest recorded use of wheat: it was being made four thousand years ago, and it is theorized that ancient civilizations boiled wheat kernels and then sun-dried them. The process produced a different—and desirable—flavor, and the grain was more resistant to mold. More recently, it has been discovered that the process also shifts desirable vitamins and minerals from the outer layers of the seed to the endosperm, the primary constituent of white flour, thus enriching it. In baking tests, the dough absorbed much more water than conventional dough, and we did not think the heavy bread would rise. But it rose rapidly and produced a loaf with an unusual and delicious flavor.

Soy Flour

Over the years, many friends have urged us to extol the health benefits of sourdoughs as a means to get more home bakers involved. However, we have always felt that the charisma and pleasure of traditional sourdough baking was more than sufficient to promote sourdoughs. There usually is little difference between sourdough's health benefits and the benefits of recipes with the same ingredients baked with commercial yeast.

Among the health, promoting ingredients used in breads (sourdough or otherwise) is soy flour. This flour is made from ground soybeans, and is not a grain. One of my professors when I was enrolled in graduate school at Cornell University was Dr. Clive McCay. He was a leader in animal nutrition and pioneered the studies of low-calorie intake in rats that produced longer life spans. In 1955, he and his wife published the first edition of *The Cornell Bread Book*. When asked to improve the diet at New York State mental hospitals, he developed the Cornell bread formula, which was supplemented with soy flour, nonfat dried milk, and wheat germ. Why soy? Soy flour is a rich protein concentrate with over 40 percent protein, but slightly deficient in methionine. When added to wheat flour, which has plenty of that amino acid but is deficient in the amino acid lysine, it produces a balanced protein comparable to meat protein. The breads (with butter) sustained McCay's rats through succeeding generations without additional food. The McCays describe methods for home bakers to produce their enriched breads by adding one tablespoon of soy flour, one tablespoon of nonfat dried milk, and one teaspoon of wheat germ for each cup (140 g) of wheat flour. When we tried this, it performed very well in every respect.

Wheat Gluten

Arrowhead Mills (among others) produces a product that is quite useful to increase the leavening potential of gluten-deficient flours, such as the rye varieties. Gluten is extracted from wheat flour through a water-washing procedure, yielding a fine white concentrated gluten. Arrowhead (whose product is called Vital Gluten) recommends $1^1/_2$ teaspoons per cup (140 g) of flour for whole grain breads.

Water

Contrary to much published advice, trace metals in water usually have no deleterious effect on breads, nor do fluoride additives. High iron concentrations in water also are of no consequence except for some effect on flavor. One potential problem is chlorine. We have never had a problem using chlorinated water, but others have reported that avoiding water with chlorine has solved problems with their sourdough baking.

Many of the recipes in this book specify warm water. "Warm" here means any temperature from 75° to 85°F (24° to 29°C). Hotter water may endanger the yeast, while colder water will slow the leavening process.

Salt

Salt has a stabilizing effect on yeast fermentation and a toughening effect on gluten. It is, incidentally, a required dough constituent under FDA standards, although salt-free bread is permitted for individuals on low-sodium diets. Almost all recipes in this book specify one or two teaspoons of salt, but it is not an essential ingredient. We also do not think sea salt has any special advantages.

Milk

Most commercially baked white breads in the United States are made with some form of milk, usually nonfat dried milk. In fact, the baking industry is the largest single consumer of this product in the country. Dried buttermilk, dried whole milk, and several whey products are used in commercial breads. The home baker has any number of options of dried and fresh milk available. The recipes in this book that call for milk all use 2 percent (reduced fat) milk, but almost any milk or milk substitute is acceptable. Remember, milk may contain antibiotics and trace amounts of disinfectants used to sterilize milking equipment. As an ingredient in bread, these contaminants may have a very slight chance of being deleterious to the organisms in your sourdough culture.

Fats

Lard, butter, oils, and margarine can generally be used interchangeably. Vegetable oils are convenient to use, while many bakers believe butter gives a better loaf texture. Fats and oils increase loaf volume, prevent crust cracking, enhance keeping qualities, and improve slicing qualities. We use them sparingly.

Sweeteners

When a recipe lists sugar, most bakers use white sugar. But many other sweeteners can be substituted, including brown sugar, corn syrups, and honey. Sugar is a yeast nutrient, although its primary function in bread making is to influence flavor. Yeasts use the carbohydrates and starch in flour as their primary energy source, and an excess of added sugar will actually inhibit, not stimulate, yeast fermentation.

Specialty Ingredients and Substitutions

Today's baker has a delicious selection of specialty baking ingredients available from around the world. From gourmet shops and health food stores one can get exotic spices, unusual flours, foreign nuts and berries, seeds, cheeses, and flavorings that make bread flavoring possibilities almost endless.

One of the major advantages of doing your own baking is your ability to adjust the recipes to your own health standards. High-fiber grains such as oats may be added to many of the recipes. Steel-cut oats, for example, produce a unique texture and distinctive flavor. To eliminate cholesterol, oil may be substituted for butter, or fat may not even be added. Many people who once enjoyed baking bread have given it up because the temptation of hot bread was too hard on their diets. However, a slice of most home-baked sourdough breads contains no cholesterol and less than 150 calories. For a healthful and durable high-calorie, high-energy snack for kids, athletes, or backpackers, add nuts, seeds, raisins, dates, wheat germ, and anything else you want.

THREE

Putting It All Together

AS YOU EMBARK on your work with sourdoughs, you'll experience both success and frustration. Just remember that there is more art (thank goodness) than science in baking as our ancestors did, and the artist learns by doing. But don't forget why you're here. Sourdoughs are for fun and personal satisfaction. Your first efforts may produce neither, but if you demand a real sourdough, it will come.

We home bakers have an enormous advantage over commercial bakers: we can afford to let our doughs ferment while we sleep until they are really ready, not half ready. It is difficult to buy a sourdough bread that isn't flavored with vinegar or a variety of chemicals to simulate the real thing. You and I bake it in our kitchens with just wild sourdough cultures, flour, water, and time. What we bake is far better than almost anything we buy.

When I first wrote *World Sourdoughs from Antiquity*, I emphasized activating dried cultures and culture preparation, or proofing, because they are critical in getting the organisms of the culture growing and reproducing. This is a chore almost unique to home bakers, since the challenge to artisan and commercial bakers is to keep their cultures growing at a constant rate—they bake daily or several times a day, usually seven days a week. If you and I bake once a week, it's probably more frequently than the average home baker, and then the culture goes back to the refrigerator and become semidormant. The next time we use it, we have to get it back up to speed. The first of the three proofs we use, the culture proof, does just that.

Some Notes on Equipment

Some bakers advocate using wooden spoons for mixing dough to avoid contamination with toxic trace metals. With modern utensils, this sort of contamination is unlikely to occur. Wooden spoons are pleasant to grip but difficult to use for heavy mixing, as they are prone to snap at the handle. Large stainless steel mixing spoons are well suited to the job, but individual preference should dictate your choice. Stainless steel or aluminum mixing bowls are also acceptable. They do not contaminate sourdoughs during the mixing or proofing periods. Heavy-duty plastic bowls are also very satisfactory.

Loaf pans and baking sheets come in every size and shape. We use metal pans and baking sheets with nonstick surfaces, which do not need to be greased before each use. If glass baking pans are used, the oven temperature should be reduced by 25°F (4°C). For loaves using about 4 cups (560 g) of flour, use $8^1/_2$ by $4^1/_2$ by $2^1/_2$-inch/ $1^1/_2$-pound (22 by 11 by 7 cm/680 g) pans. In this book, most of the recipes for shaped loaves are designed to yield $1^1/_2$-pound (680 g) loaves: if your bread pans are a little bigger or smaller, take that into account when judging whether a loaf has risen enough in the pan during the final, loaf proof. A willow basket for the last rise produces an interesting artisan loaf. Oven-safe stoneware vessels, such as La Cloche, are also popular (see page 54 for a recipe designed for using a La Cloche).

A number of the recipes here suggest using a preheated baking stone as a baking surface. These are especially useful for breads requiring high, even temperatures, such as pizzas and flatbreads, though they can be successfully used with many loaves.

The Proofing Box

A proofing box made from an inexpensive Styrofoam cooler will accurately regulate proofing temperatures, which is important for achieving the desired flavors, leavening, and sourness. Select a cooler large enough to fit upside down over your large mixing bowls—approximately 20 by 13 by 11 inches (50 by 33 by 28 cm). Turn the cooler upside down and install a standard porcelain lightbulb socket *inside* near the center of the bottom (now the top) of the cooler, with an ordinary rheostat (dimmer switch) in the power cord. Use a 25-watt lightbulb and an accurate thermometer to measure the interior temperature. We use an outdoor thermometer. We've found that heating pads, incubators, or aquarium heaters are not as efficient as this system.

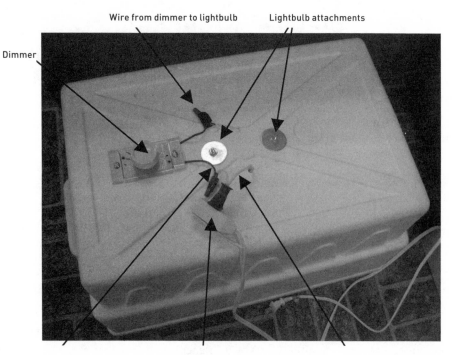

Dimmer

Wire from dimmer to lightbulb

Lightbulb attachments

Wire from power plug to dimmer

Power plug connected to power cord

Wire from power plug to lightbulb

Inside view

Steps in Proofing

After activation, a sourdough goes through three proofing stages on its way to becoming a bread. First, the active culture is proofed to greatly increase the number of organisms; then the dough is given a lengthy proof after kneading, allowing both yeast and lactobacilli to multiply throughout the dough; and finally the shaped loaves are proofed to maximize both leavening and flavor.

ACTIVATING A DRY CULTURE

Activation is a sort of preproofing step, which converts a dried, dormant culture into a mass of active sourdough organisms ready to be further prepared for use in the "culture proof" stage described below. Activation is achieved by simply adding flour and water to the dried culture (which is a mixture of concentrated organisms and the flour in which they were grown) and proofing for three to five days. This is something you'll do only once, when you first acquire a dried sourdough culture.

Start by thoroughly mixing all the dried culture (which contains approximately $^1/_4$ cup/35 g of flour) with $^3/_4$ cup (105 g) of unbleached all-purpose flour and $^3/_4$ cup (180 ml) of warm water in a 1-quart (1 liter) widemouthed canning jar. The culture should be the consistency of thick pancake batter. Place the jar in a warm place (about 90°F/32°C) and proof for about 24 hours. A proofing box is useful at this stage (see page 26); if you use one, check the temperature of the proofing box with a reliable outdoor thermometer. This high starting temperature promotes the growth of the lactobacilli and thus increases acid production. High acidity helps prevent contamination of the active culture by nonsourdough organisms present in most flour, most of which do not thrive in an acid environment.

At the end of 24 hours, a few bubbles may appear in the culture as the first sign of growth and activity. Now reduce the proofing temperature to about 70°F (21°C). This lower temperature slows the bacterial growth and acid production—important at this stage as too much acidity inhibits the growth of the yeast. Continue feeding the culture every 12 to 24 hours for 3 to 5 days: feed with 1 cup (140 g) of flour and enough water (up to $^3/_4$ cup/180 ml) to maintain the thick pancake-batter consistency. It will be necessary to discard about half of the mixture before each feeding or the jar will overflow. Discarding dilutes the culture and helps reduce acid buildup. This is a good time to divide the culture into two jars—one for a backup in case of an accident with the other. After dividing into an additional jar, feed both jars.

Sometimes the culture becomes quite active in the first 24 hours. This could be a sign of contamination, but if the culture has a pleasant odor and continues to respond when fed, it is a good culture and can be retained. If the odor is unpleasant, follow the directions for washing a culture below.

When foam and bubbles increase the culture's volume by about 3 inches (8 cm) within 2 to 3 hours of its last feeding, the culture is fully active and can be used or refrigerated until needed.

During refrigeration, as the culture becomes semidormant, a layer of clear tan or brown fluid forms on the surface. This is the "hooch": it's perfectly normal, and it should be stirred back in when the culture is used.

Culture Container

A 1-quart (1 liter) widemouthed glass canning jar is recommended for activation and maintenance of cultures. These jars perform an essential function. Each time additional flour is added, the subsequent activity of lactobacilli makes the culture slightly more acidic. Repeat feedings in a larger container will create excessive acidity and inhibit the wild yeast. In contrast, using quart (liter) jars means you must discard part of the activating culture at each feeding or the mixture will overflow the jar. This dilutes the acidity slightly at each feeding. In addition, with glass jars you can see activity inside the developing culture. The jar lid should not be tightened, but put on loosely.

"Washing" a Culture

During the first step of activation, the amount of flour added to the culture is almost three times the amount in the dried culture. It is at this point that contamination by nonsourdough organisms present in most flour sometimes, though rarely, occurs. Contamination is more likely when the initial activating temperature is not high enough, causing slow acidification by the lactobacilli. Evidence of contamination usually appears in the first 24 hours: the culture may produce sufficient bubbles and foam to suggest that the culture is activating prematurely, and it may give off an unpleasant odor. Contamination can usually be corrected by "washing" the culture to dilute the contaminating organisms (as well as the good ones) and starting the 90°F (32°C) proof again, giving the lactobacilli another opportunity to acidify the culture.

To "wash" a culture, mix thoroughly and discard all but about 1 cup (240 ml) of the culture. Then fill the jar almost to the top with warm (75° to 85°F/24° to 29°C) water while stirring vigorously. Again discard all but about 1 cup (240 ml). Now feed it $^2/_3$ cup (90 g) of flour and enough water to maintain the consistency of thick pancake batter. Proof at 90°F (32°C) for 24 hours. There should be a marked reduction in activity as contamination is reduced. After 24 hours, feed $^2/_3$ cup (90 g) of flour and enough water (about $^1/_2$ cup/120 ml) to maintain the consistency. Reduce the proofing temperature to about 70°F (21°C) and continue discarding and feeding as above every 12 hours at this lower temperature. When normal fermentation takes over and the culture becomes fully active, the layer of foam and bubbles will reach almost to the jar top 2 to 4 hours after the last feeding. The culture is then ready to use or refrigerate. If the culture does not begin to revive in 2 to 3 days, the washing process should be repeated.

FULLY ACTIVE CULTURE

One of the most critical factors for success with sourdoughs is the fully active culture. For well over a hundred years, commercial sourdough bakers rebuilt their cultures several times each day. Some still do. However, many home bakers bake less than once a week, and their refrigerated cultures are always partially dormant, depending on how long they have been in the refrigerator. But the lactobacilli always remain somewhat active, and the culture becomes increasingly acidic the longer it rests. When a refrigerated culture is warmed and fed flour and water, the organisms begin to reactivate, but the activity of the wild yeast is often inhibited by the increased acidity of the culture.

To reduce a culture's acidity, when you take it out of the refrigerator, fill the culture jar with warm water while stirring vigorously. Leave slightly more than 1 cup (240 ml) in the jar and discard the excess. (If you will be baking more than one loaf and so anticipate needing more than one jar of culture, use the excess to build additional culture in the following steps.)

Feed the culture in the jar $^2/_3$ cup (90 g) of flour and sufficient water to restore the consistency of thick pancake batter. The jar should now be slightly more than half full (we are assuming a 1-quart/1 liter jar).

Proof at 70° to 75°F (21° to 24°C). If the culture has been in the refrigerator for less than 2 weeks, it is only mildly dormant and will usually become fully active in approximately 2 to 4 hours when proofed at room temperature. If it does not respond well, an additional feeding may be necessary. As soon as it forms foam and bubbles that increase the total volume by about 2 inches (5 cm) in a quart (liter) jar within 2 to 4 hours of the last feeding, it is fully active and ready for use in the culture proof (see below). If the culture has been refrigerated for more than 2 weeks, this procedure may have to be repeated.

Proofing Terminology

Many bakers and authors refer to their sourdough cultures as "starters," since a small amount of pure culture is always retained to "start" the next batch. We use the two terms—starter and culture—interchangeably.

Throughout this book, we use the term "proof." According to *Webster's*, it means "to test the activeness of yeast." Early bakers used the term because they were "proving" the dough—making sure it would rise. In current usage, it refers to the process of yeast fermenting flour and water to produce dough and later to make the dough rise.

CULTURE PROOF

Warming and feeding for an hour or two is usually not enough to prepare a refrigerated culture for use in a sourdough. The creation of a "culture proof" allows you to infuse your culture with a massive inoculum of sourdough organisms, optimizing flavor and leavening.

Start with a fully active culture (see opposite page). Stir it vigorously and put half in another jar. To each jar, add $^2/_3$ cup (90 g) of flour and enough water to maintain the thick pancake-batter consistency (about $^1/_2$ cup/120 ml). Proof for 8 to 12 hours.

We like to proof at 65° to 70°F (18° to 21°C) for the first 2 to 3 hours, followed by 6 to 10 hours at 80° to 85°F (26° to 29°C). This results in a good concentration of both yeast and bacteria, producing good flavor, leavening, and sourness.

If you choose to proof at a higher temperature of 85° to 90°F (29° to 32°C), the culture will become moderately acidic and the yeast inhibited. This may cause the culture to appear flat and inactive at the end of the proof, but it is now ready for use in the dough proof with a good concentration of lactobacilli. The flavor and sourness of this culture will be good, the leavening moderate to poor. In contrast, when the proofing temperature is between 65° and 70°F (18° and 21°C), the flavor and leavening will be excellent but the sourness mild.

You will need to experiment to discover what works best for your environment and your tastes. For example, when Jean would bake in Hawaii she learned that in warm kitchens above 80°F (26°C) where it is not possible to achieve 65° to 70°F (18° to 21°C) for part of the proofing time, it may be necessary to reduce the length of time of both the culture proof and the dough proof.

If the dough seems quite active when the loaves are formed, but they either do not rise or they retract when baked, it is probably because the dough is acidic, and during the loaf proof this acidity reaches the point where the yeast is inhibited. An unusually sour loaf will verify that this is what happened; by trial and error, the right balance in a warm environment can be achieved. If you are using a proofing box during the culture proof, another solution is to turn off the lightbulb and put blue ice in the proofing box. This works quite well to maintain lower temperatures.

Dough Consistency

The amounts of flour and water listed in the various proofs and recipes are specified primarily as guidelines for the beginner: don't get unnecessarily hung up on the math. Dough consistency is best judged based on the baker's past experience. The basic sourdough recipe (page 38), for example, provides just the right consistency (ratio of flour to water) for our environment, but you may have to experiment a bit.

When kneading, if the dough is too dry or stiff, add more water. If it is too thin, add more flour. When a perfectly formed loaf of dough becomes a flattened pancake just before or during baking, the consistency was too thin and more flour was needed. Sourdoughs kneaded by hand are much more tolerant than sourdoughs in machines: proper dough consistency in baking machines is essential for proper kneading.

You can control the texture of the finished product by changing the amount of water in the dough until an open crumb is achieved, as the crumb depends largely on the consistency (wetness) of the dough. Increasing the water in a recipe by small increments means the crumb will be more open with larger holes, but don't add too much: a very wet dough may not rise as well.

DOUGH PROOF

After the culture has been fully activated and proofed, it's time to make and proof the dough. Take the amount of culture specified in the recipe from the culture proof and knead it together with the additional ingredients in the recipe (see below), either by hand or, if the volume is not too large, in a bread machine (see page 152 for kneading in a bread machine.) To store the rest of your culture for another time, feed the remaining culture a cup (140 g) of flour and ³/₄ cup (180 ml) of water, proof for an hour or two, and refrigerate.

After kneading the dough, proof it overnight (for 8 to 12 hours) at room temperature in a large bowl (or in the machine pan taken out of the machine) covered with plastic wrap and secured by a rubber band. The volume will greatly increase; it should rise to the top of the machine pan. This fermentation, or dough proof, increases the number of organisms in the dough and allows the flavor to develop.

After the proof, use a spatula to gently ease the dough from the container to a floured board, and allow it to rest for 30 minutes to relax the gluten. During the 30-minute rest, the dough mass should retain, with only modest changes, the irregular shape it assumed when it was transferred to the board. If it spreads out, with marked flattening, it is probably necessary to knead in additional flour before moving on to the next step of shaping the dough.

Kneading 101

There has probably been more written about kneading than about any other aspect of bread making. We'll add just a few observations: it is hard to do it wrong; it is hard to do too much; and it takes a little experience to become comfortable doing it and to know when to quit. Most of us enjoy kneading. It's one of those mind-releasing exercises that contributes to the overall satisfaction of making bread. And it is certainly easier to work stiff dough with your hands than it is with a large spoon.

Kneading should begin when the dough becomes too stiff to handle easily with a spoon and starts to fall away from the sides of the bowl. At this point, turn it onto a floured board—or, in the phrase seen in every baking book, "a well-floured board." With sourdoughs, which sometimes are a little sticky, we frequently use an entire cup (140 g) to cover the bread board before turning the dough out of the bowl. This extra flour is very helpful. Gather the soft dough into a loose ball and start to work it back and forth with the palm and heel of your hand. Flatten the ball and fold over the far edge to fill in the depression you just made, then push it down again. Between pushes, rotate the dough about a quarter turn so that it all gets an equal share of kneading. As you push it back and forth, the dough will pick up flour from the board and from your hands. As it becomes sticky, work more flour into the dough, sprinkling more on the board if necessary. Continue until the dough quits picking up flour from the board and begins to stiffen perceptibly. It will develop a "rebound" feeling and a satiny sheen and smooth texture. If the dough is not stiff enough, it will droop and fall over the edge of the pan when it rises; French loaves will spread sideways, producing a flat loaf instead of a plump one. If the dough is too stiff and dry, the loaves will split as they rise, allowing the leavening gases to escape prematurely.

Can you knead too much? Probably not if you are doing it by hand. You can over-knead if you are using a power mixer. Overkneaded dough will "slacken," and the resulting gluten will be of poor quality, letting a portion of the leavening gases escape. Moist dough can be sticky and difficult to handle, making machine kneading desirable. However, power mixers and food processors vary markedly in their ability to handle sourdoughs, which are far more tenacious than bread doughs made with commercial yeast. Follow the manufacturer's instructions for your mixer carefully, but don't be surprised if sourdoughs overload your equipment. We have experienced significant problems even with good, heavy-duty equipment.

SHAPING

After the 30-minute rest, flatten the dough slightly, retaining the contained air bubbles as much as possible. Then lift a portion from the periphery and pull it toward the center. Continue this around the dough mass, forming a rough ball. As the individual segments are pulled toward the center, a uniform surface under tension forms a "skin" of sorts around the ball. Complete the process by pinching the ends of the segments together at the center. Gently move the ball, or loaf, to the final proofing container with the seam side up if you're proofing in a willow basket, or down if you're placing it on a baking surface to proof. If desired, shape the loaf further; for example, into a long, narrow French loaf or a round boule.

If you are using bread pans, the recipes are designed for $8^{1}/_{2}$ by $4^{1}/_{2}$ by $2^{1}/_{2}$-inch/$1^{1}/_{2}$-pound (22 by 11 by 7 cm/680 g) pans. Usually you can expect a sourdough to at least double in volume. If you use larger pans, your dough, even if it doubles in volume, may not fill the larger pan and may seem to not rise sufficiently.

LOAF PROOF

After placing the shaped loaf in a bread pan or other baking container or a willow basket or, for French loaves, on a baking sheet, proof for 2 to 4 hours, until it reaches nearly to the top of the pan or doubles in bulk.

If the loaf is proofed at room temperature, the flavor and leavening will be good but the sourness mild. Proofing at higher temperatures (85° to 90°F/29° to 32°C) will produce a more sour loaf with good flavor but decreased leavening. If you proof the loaf at room temperature for the first hour and then raise the temperature to 90°F (32°C) for the second hour (and if the culture was proofed at 80° to 85°F/26° to 29°C during the last part of the culture proof), it will produce a much more sour loaf with only slightly decreased leavening.

SLASHING

Slashing the surface of the dough just before putting the loaf in the oven produces an attractive crust appearance and provides an escape route for expanding gases during baking. Razor blades are an ideal tool for slashing: use a blade that is sharp enough to cut through the unbaked crust without tearing it. Allow the dough surface to dry briefly so that the slash is easier to perform without dragging wet dough on the blade. Make the cuts about $^1/_8$ to $^1/_4$ inch (3 to 6 mm) deep. The slash is rarely deeper than $^1/_2$ inch (12 mm). If it is made at a 45-degree angle to the dough surface, it will form a curled ridge during baking called the "shag." This takes practice.

BAKING

Preheating an oven before baking is a time-honored practice. But we have been surprised to find that starting the baking process in a cold oven results in a better "oven spring." If you do this, increase the baking time by how long it takes your oven to reach whatever temperature you set for baking. For example, our oven takes approximately 10 minutes to reach 375°F (190°C). Place the baking container or sheet with its shaped loaf in a cool oven set for 375°F (190°C). Start the oven and bake for 70 minutes. At the start of baking—usually just after the oven comes up to full baking temperature—watch the loaf suddenly expand as the gases in the dough heat up. This expansion is called "oven spring." If the consistency is just right, the sudden expansion will be double or triple the usual expansion: we call that "ballooning." When you first see a dough balloon, it will actually startle you. It takes practice and record keeping to consistently achieve this exceptional rise. Alternatively, you may bake the loaf on a baking stone preheated to 450°F (230°C) for 40 minutes.

Supply steam by placing boiling water in a pan below the loaf or spritzing the oven—not the loaves—with water every 5 minutes for the first 15 minutes of baking. This creates a chewy crust (see below).

When bread is taken from the oven after baking, it should be removed from the pan and allowed to cool on a wire rack. If left in the pan, it will become moist and soggy. Most breads should not be sliced until 15 to 20 minutes after being taken from the oven: this time is important to the final texture.

Crust Texture

The texture of the crust can be modified by different treatments before and during baking. Brushing with cold water just before baking produces a harder crust. French breads usually have a chewy crust, which is produced by placing a shallow pan of boiling water in the oven for the first ten minutes to simulate a steam oven. We spray the oven with water in a mister several times at five-minute intervals just as baking starts, and the resulting crusts are really terrific. A softer crust will result if the loaves are brushed with melted butter or oil before baking.

For a glossy, hard coating, use 1 teaspoon of cornstarch in $1/2$ cup (120 ml) of water: heat the mixture to boiling, then let it cool and apply it with a brush just before baking. A glaze made from a well-beaten egg produces a golden brown crust. For a deep brown, try brushing with milk. Any of these glazes can be used just before baking and once or twice during baking if desired.

Freezing and Thawing Breads

Baked sourdough breads maintain their flavor, aroma, and freshness very well when frozen for several months. As soon as the loaves have completely cooled, double-wrap them in plastic and aluminum foil and place in the freezer. Thaw the frozen loaf overnight at room temperature, or place unwrapped in an oven preheated to 350°F (175°C) for 15 minutes, or put in a microwave oven on high power for up to 4 minutes, rotating frequently.

FOUR

Recipes

THESE BREAD RECIPES contain many different healthful grains and tasty add-ins. We recommend that you start by baking the Basic Sourdough Bread recipe, which serves as an introduction to our unique culture proof step and the subsequent effects of timing and temperature variations on the final result. Once you've mastered this basic recipe, you will be ready to bake any sourdough recipe in this book.

We like to mix and knead the dough in a bread machine, as it is easier to judge the consistency, but we usually remove it for shaping and baking (see chapter 5 for a description of this method). Any of the following recipes can be kneaded in the machine if they yield one loaf.

Basic Sourdough Bread

Try this basic recipe first, to familiarize yourself with the three proofs needed for each recipe and to discover which culture proof and loaf proof variations create your preferred flavor and leavening. Note that you must complete the first proof, the Culture Proof, *before you begin making the dough in the recipe. Master this recipe, and you can use what you learn to adjust any of the recipes that follow to your taste.* MAKES ONE 1½-POUND (680 G) LOAF

1 cup (240 ml) culture from the Culture Proof (page 31)	1 teaspoon salt
1 cup (240 ml) water	3½ cups (490 g) unbleached all-purpose flour

DOUGH PROOF Pour the culture into a mixing bowl. Stir the water and salt into the culture with a mixing spoon. Add the flour a cup (140 g) at a time until the dough is too stiff to mix by hand. Turn out onto a floured board and knead in the remaining flour until the dough is smooth and satiny.

Or mix and knead all of the ingredients for a maximum of 25 minutes in a bread machine or other mixer (see page 152).

Proof the dough overnight (8 to 12 hours) at room temperature, about 70°F (21°C), in a large bowl covered with plastic wrap (or leave in the machine pan, removed from the machine, securing the plastic wrap with a rubber band). During this time, the dough should double in size in the covered bowl, or rise to the top of the machine pan. After the proof, use a spatula to gently ease the dough out onto a floured board.

Allow the dough to rest for 30 minutes. If marked flattening occurs during this time, knead in additional flour before shaping.

After the 30-minute rest, shape the dough. Flatten it slightly, then lift a portion from the periphery and pull it toward the center. Continue this around the dough mass to form a rough ball (see page 34), then pat and pull into the loaf shape you desire.

LOAF PROOF Place the shaped loaf in a bread pan or other baking container, in a willow basket, or, for French loaves, on a baking sheet. Cover and proof (either at room temperature or in the warmer atmosphere of a proofing box, depending on your preferred temperature) for 2 to 4 hours until it has doubled in bulk or reached nearly to the top of the bread pan. Remember that proofing at higher temperatures

(90°F/32°C) will produce a more sour loaf with good flavor but decreased leavening. Proofing at room temperature will yield good leavening and mild sourness. Proofing at room temperature for the first hour, and then at 90°F (32°C) until risen will yield a moderately sour loaf with only slightly decreased leavening.

BAKING Just before putting the loaf in the oven, slash the surface of the dough several times with a razor blade. Place the pan with its shaped, proofed loaf in a cool oven, then turn the temperature to 375°F (190°C) and bake for 70 minutes. Or transfer the loaf to a preheated baking stone in a 450°F (230°C) oven and bake for 40 minutes. For a firm, chewy crust, place a pan of boiling water below the loaf or spritz the oven with water every 5 minutes for 15 minutes while the oven is at baking temperature. When the loaf is baked, remove it from the pan and let cool on a wire rack for at least 15 to 20 minutes before slicing.

San Francisco Sourdough

It seems incredible that the ingredients in this well-known bread are so few: a wild culture, flour, water, and salt. We use our authentic Original San Francisco culture, which will produce the flavor and texture that we know as San Francisco sourdough. To customize its sourness and leavening, refer to chapter 3 for variations in timing and temperature during proofing (page 31) and baking (page 35). MAKES ONE 1½-POUND (680 G) LOAF

1 cup (240 ml) culture from the
  Culture Proof (page 31)
1½ teaspoons salt

1 cup (240 ml) water
3½ cups (490 g) unbleached
  all-purpose flour

DOUGH PROOF Pour the culture into a mixing bowl. Dissolve the salt in the water and stir it into the culture. Add the flour a cup (140 g) at a time and stir until it is too stiff to mix with a spoon. Turn out onto a floured board and knead in the remaining flour until the dough is smooth and satiny.

Or mix and knead all of the ingredients for a maximum of 25 minutes in a bread machine or other mixer (see page 152).

Proof the dough overnight (8 to 12 hours) at room temperature, about 70°F (21°C), in a large bowl covered with plastic wrap (or leave in the machine pan, removed from the machine, securing the plastic wrap with a rubber band). During this time, the dough should double in size in the covered bowl, or rise to the top of the machine pan. After the proof, use a spatula to gently ease the dough out onto a floured board. Allow the dough to rest for 30 minutes. If marked flattening occurs during this time, knead in additional flour before shaping.

LOAF PROOF After the 30-minute rest, shape the dough. Flatten it slightly, then lift a portion from the periphery and pull it toward the center. Continue this around the dough mass to form a rough ball (see page 34), then shape as a French loaf by gently patting the dough into a rough rectangle, then folding over and pressing the edges together to make a seam.

Place the shaped loaf, seam side down, on a baking sheet and proof for 2 to 4 hours until it doubles in bulk. For a good combination of sourness and leavening, proof the loaf for the first hour at room temperature and then at 85° to 90°F (29° to 32°C) in a proofing box.

BAKING Place the baking sheet with its shaped loaf in a cool oven, then turn the temperature to 375°F (190°C) and bake for 70 minutes. Or transfer the loaf to a preheated baking stone in a 450°F (230°C) oven and bake for 40 minutes. For a firm, chewy crust, place a pan of boiling water below the loaf or spritz the oven with water every 5 minutes for 15 minutes while the oven is at baking temperature. When the loaf is baked, remove it from the pan and let cool on a wire rack for at least 15 to 20 minutes before slicing.

French White Bread

This is a conventional white loaf bread—delicious but different from the well-known French loaf. MAKES ONE 1½-POUND (680 G) LOAF

1 cup (240 ml) culture from the
   Culture Proof (page 31)
1 egg, beaten
1 teaspoon salt
1 teaspoon sugar
1 cup (240 ml) milk
2 tablespoons (30 g) melted butter
3½ cups (490 g) unbleached
   all-purpose flour

GLAZE
¼ cup (60 ml) milk
Poppy seed

DOUGH PROOF Pour the culture into a mixing bowl. Add the beaten egg, salt, sugar, milk, and melted butter to the culture and mix. Add the flour a cup (140 g) at a time and stir until the dough is too stiff to mix by hand. Turn out onto a floured board and knead in the remaining flour until the dough is smooth and satiny.

Or mix and knead all of the ingredients for a maximum of 25 minutes in a bread machine or other mixer (see page 152).

Proof the dough overnight (8 to 12 hours) at room temperature, about 70°F (21°C), in a large bowl covered with plastic wrap (or leave in the machine pan, removed from the machine, securing the plastic wrap with a rubber band). During this time, the dough should double in size in the covered bowl, or rise to the top of the machine pan. After the proof, use a spatula to gently ease the dough out onto a floured board.

Allow the dough to rest for 30 minutes. If marked flattening occurs during this time, knead in additional flour before shaping.

LOAF PROOF After the 30-minute rest, shape the dough. Flatten it slightly, then lift a portion from the periphery and pull it toward the center. Continue this around the dough mass to form a rough ball (see page 34), then pat and pull into the loaf shape you desire.

Place the shaped loaf, seam side down, on a baking sheet or in a bread pan and proof for 2 to 4 hours, until it doubles in bulk or reaches nearly the top of the pan.

For a good combination of sourness and leavening, proof the loaf for the first hour at room temperature and then at 85° to 90°F (29° to 32°C) in a proofing box.

BAKING Just before putting the loaf in the oven, slash the surface of the dough several times with a razor blade, brush with milk, and sprinkle with poppy seed. Place the baking container or sheet with its shaped loaf in a cool oven, then turn the temperature to 375°F (190°C) and bake for 70 minutes. Or transfer the loaf to a preheated baking stone in a 450°F (230°C) oven and bake for 40 minutes. When the loaf is baked, remove it from the pan and let cool on a wire rack for at least 15 to 20 minutes before slicing.

Light Swedish Limpa

Limpa is a rye bread flavored with brown sugar or molasses. This one uses brown sugar, but many Austrian limpas use both. The orange rind is an absolute requirement to complement this bread's light rye flavor. Use a coarse grater to produce substantial strips and chunks of the orange rind, making sure to avoid using any of the bitter white pith. We bake it as a round loaf. MAKES ONE 1½-POUND (680 G) LOAF

1 tablespoon (15 g) butter
1 cup (240 ml) water
1 teaspoon salt
¼ cup (60 g) brown sugar
Grated zest of one orange
1½ teaspoons caraway seed

1 tablespoon fennel seed
1 cup (240 ml) culture from the
  Culture Proof (page 31)
1 cup (115 g) rye flour
2½ cups (350 g) unbleached
  all-purpose flour

DOUGH PROOF Melt the butter, then add the water to warm. Add the salt, brown sugar, zest, caraway seed, and fennel seed and stir. In a large mixing bowl, add this mixture to the culture and mix well. Add the rye flour and mix well. Add the all-purpose flour a cup (140 g) at a time until the dough is too stiff to mix with a spoon. Turn out onto a floured board and knead in the remaining flour until the dough is smooth and satiny.

Or mix and knead the butter mixture with the flours for a maximum of 25 minutes in a bread machine or other mixer (see page 152).

Proof the dough overnight (8 to 12 hours) at room temperature, about 70°F (21°C), in a large bowl covered with plastic wrap (or leave in the machine pan, removed from the machine, securing the plastic wrap with a rubber band). During this time, the dough should double in size in the covered bowl, or rise to the top of the machine pan. After the proof, use a spatula to gently ease the dough out onto a floured board.

Allow the dough to rest for 30 minutes. If marked flattening occurs during this time, knead in additional flour before shaping.

LOAF PROOF After the 30-minute rest, shape the dough. Flatten it slightly, then lift a portion from the periphery and pull it toward the center. Continue this around the dough mass to form a rough ball (see page 34), then pat and pull into the loaf shape you desire.

Place the shaped loaf, seam side down, on a baking sheet or in a round baking pan and proof for 2 to 4 hours until it doubles in bulk. For a good combination of sourness and leavening, proof the loaf for the first hour at room temperature and then at 85° to 90°F (29° to 32°C) in a proofing box.

BAKING Just before putting the loaf in the oven, slash the surface of the dough several times with a razor blade. Place the pan with its shaped, proofed loaf in a cool oven, then turn the temperature to 375°F (190°C) and bake for 70 minutes. Or transfer the loaf to a preheated baking stone in a 450°F (230°C) oven and bake for 40 minutes. When the loaf is baked, remove it from the pan and let cool on a wire rack for at least 15 to 20 minutes before slicing.

Tanya's Peasant Black Bread

Our friend Tanya says this recipe really doesn't duplicate the bread of her native Russia because of differences in flour; an investigative trip to Russia may be in order. The combination of coriander and molasses complements the sourdough flavor, so don't leave either out. MAKES ONE 1½-POUND (680 G) LOAF

1 cup (240 ml) milk	1 cup (240 ml) culture from the
1 tablespoon dark molasses	Culture Proof (page 31)
1 tablespoon vegetable oil	1 cup (115 g) rye flour
1 tablespoon sugar	1 cup (140 g) whole wheat flour
1 teaspoon salt	1½ cups (210 g) unbleached
½ teaspoon ground coriander	all-purpose flour

DOUGH PROOF In a small saucepan over moderate heat, warm the milk. Remove from the heat and add the molasses, oil, sugar, salt, and coriander; mix briefly and combine with the culture in a mixing bowl.

Add the rye flour and mix well. Add the whole wheat flour and mix well. Add the all-purpose flour ½ cup (70 g) at a time and mix until too stiff to stir with a spoon. Turn the dough out onto a floured board and knead in the remaining flour until the dough is smooth and satiny.

Or mix the milk mixture with the flours and knead in a bread machine or other mixer (see page 152) for a maximum of 25 minutes.

Proof the dough overnight (8 to 12 hours) at room temperature, about 70°F (21°C), in a large bowl covered with plastic wrap (or leave in the machine pan, removed from the machine, securing the plastic wrap with a rubber band). During this time, the dough should double in size in the covered bowl, or rise to the top of the machine pan. After the proof, use a spatula to gently ease the dough out onto a floured board.

Allow the dough to rest for 30 minutes. If marked flattening occurs during this time, knead in additional flour before shaping.

LOAF PROOF After the 30-minute rest, shape the dough. Flatten it slightly, then lift a portion from the periphery and pull it toward the center. Continue this around the dough mass to form a rough ball (see page 34), then pat and pull into the loaf shape you desire.

Place the shaped loaf, seam side down, on a baking sheet or in a bread pan and proof for 2 to 4 hours, until it doubles in bulk or reaches nearly to the top of the bread pan. For a good combination of sourness and leavening, proof the loaf for the first hour at room temperature and then at 85° to 90°F (29° to 32°C) in a proofing box.

BAKING Just before putting the loaf in the oven, slash the surface of the dough several times with a razor blade. Place the pan with its shaped, proofed loaf in a cool oven, then turn the temperature to 375°F (190°C) and bake for 70 minutes. Or transfer the loaf to a preheated baking stone in a 450°F (230°C) oven and bake for 40 minutes. When the loaf is baked, remove it from the pan and let cool on a wire rack for at least 15 to 20 minutes before slicing.

French Bread

Sourdough breads fell out of favor in French cities after the turn of the twentieth century, when commercial yeast became available. Nowadays, however, sourdoughs are back in vogue and once again prevail in the smaller bakeries of France. Much has been written about the difficulties of emulating the French bakery with its steam ovens and special brick. For an authentically firm, chewy crust without the specialized equipment, place a pan of boiling water below the loaf or spritz the oven with water every 5 minutes for 15 minutes while the oven is at baking temperature. MAKES ONE 1½-POUND (680 G) LOAF

1 cup (240 ml) culture from the
  Culture Proof (page 31)
1½ teaspoons salt
1 cup (240 ml) water

3½ cups (490 g) unbleached
  all-purpose flour
2 tablespoons white cornmeal

DOUGH PROOF Pour the culture into a mixing bowl. Dissolve the salt in the water, add to the culture, and mix well. Add the flour a cup (140 g) at a time and mix until too stiff to stir by hand. Turn out onto a floured board and knead in the remaining flour until the dough is smooth and satiny.

Or mix and knead all of the ingredients (except the cornmeal) for a maximum of 25 minutes in a bread machine or other mixer (see page 152).

Proof the dough overnight (8 to 12 hours) at room temperature, about 70°F (21°C), in a large bowl covered with plastic wrap (or leave in the machine pan, removed from the machine securing, the plastic wrap with a rubber band). During this time, the dough should double in size in the covered bowl, or rise to the top of the machine pan. After the proof, use a spatula to gently ease the dough out onto a floured board.

Allow the dough to rest for 30 minutes. If marked flattening occurs during this time, knead in additional flour before shaping.

LOAF PROOF After the 30-minute rest, shape the dough. Flatten it slightly, then lift a portion from the periphery and pull it toward the center. Continue this around the dough mass to form a rough ball (see page 34), then shape as a French loaf by gently patting the dough into a rough rectangle then folding over and pressing the edges together to make a seam.

Sprinkle a baking sheet with the cornmeal and place the shaped dough, seam side down, on the sheet. Proof for 2 to 4 hours, until it doubles in bulk. For a good combination of sourness and leavening, proof the loaf for the first hour at room temperature and then at 85° to 90°F (29° to 32°C) in a proofing box.

BAKING Just before baking, make diagonal slashes in the crust with a razor blade. Place the baking sheet with its shaped loaf in a cool oven, then turn the temperature to 375°F (190°C) and bake for 70 minutes. Or transfer the loaf to a preheated baking stone in a 450°F (230°C) oven and bake for 40 minutes. When the loaf is baked, remove it from the pan and let cool on a wire rack for at least 15 to 20 minutes before slicing.

Whole Wheat Bread

This is a terrific basic whole wheat loaf with excellent texture and flavor. MAKES ONE
1¹/₂-POUND (680 G) LOAF

1 cup (240 ml) culture from the
    Culture Proof (page 31)
1¹/₂ teaspoons salt
1 tablespoon sugar
1 cup (240 ml) milk

1 tablespoon (15 g) melted butter
1¹/₂ cups (210 g) whole wheat flour
2 cups (280 g) unbleached
    all-purpose flour

DOUGH PROOF Pour the culture into a mixing bowl. Add the salt, sugar, milk, and butter to the culture and mix well. Add the whole wheat flour and mix well. Add the all-purpose flour a cup (140 g) at a time until the dough is too stiff to mix by hand. Turn out onto a floured board and knead in the remaining flour until smooth and satiny.

Or mix and knead all of the ingredients for a maximum of 25 minutes in a bread machine or other mixer (see page 152).

Proof the dough overnight (8 to 12 hours) at room temperature, about 70°F (21°C), in a large bowl covered with plastic wrap (or leave in the machine pan, removed from the machine, securing the plastic wrap with a rubber band). During this time, the dough should double in size in the covered bowl, or rise to the top of the machine pan. After the proof, use a spatula to gently ease the dough out onto a floured board.

Allow the dough to rest for 30 minutes. If marked flattening occurs during this time, knead in additional flour before shaping.

LOAF PROOF After the 30-minute rest, shape the dough. Flatten it slightly, then lift a portion from the periphery and pull it toward the center. Continue this around the dough mass to form a rough ball (see page 34), then pat and pull into the loaf shape you desire.

Place the shaped loaf, seam side down, on a baking sheet or in a bread pan and proof for 2 to 4 hours, until it doubles in bulk or reaches nearly to the top of the bread pan. For a good combination of sourness and leavening, proof the loaf for the first hour at room temperature and then at 85° to 90°F (29° to 32°C) in a proofing box.

BAKING Place the pan with its shaped, proofed loaf in a cool oven, then turn the temperature to 375°F (190°C) and bake for 70 minutes. When the loaf is baked, remove it from the pan and let cool on a wire rack for at least 15 to 20 minutes before slicing.

Date Bread

This recipe features sweet, dense dates in a loaf leavened by wild yeast. This is a heavy dough and cannot be hurried. MAKES ONE 2-POUND (900 G) LOAF

1 cup (240 ml) culture from the
   Culture Proof (page 31)
1 cup (240 ml) water
2 tablespoons oil
1 cup (150 g) chopped dates

1 cup (100 g) chopped nuts
1/4 cup (50 g) sugar
1 teaspoon salt
3 1/2 cups (490 g) unbleached
   all-purpose flour

DOUGH PROOF Pour the culture into a mixing bowl. Add the water, oil, dates, nuts, sugar, and salt and mix well. Add the flour a cup (140 g) at a time until the dough is too stiff to mix by hand. Turn out onto a floured board and knead in the remaining flour until the dough is smooth and satiny.

Proof the dough overnight (8 to 12 hours) at room temperature, about 70°F (21°C), in a large bowl covered with plastic wrap. During this time, the dough should double in size. After the proof, use a spatula to gently ease the dough out onto a floured board.

Allow the dough to rest for 30 minutes. If marked flattening occurs during this time, knead in additional flour before shaping.

LOAF PROOF After the 30-minute rest, shape the dough. Flatten it slightly, then lift a portion from the periphery and pull it toward the center. Continue this around the dough mass to form a rough ball (see page 34), then pat and pull into the loaf shape you desire.

Place the shaped loaf, seam side down, on a baking sheet or in a bread pan and proof for 2 to 4 hours, until it doubles in bulk or reaches nearly to the top of the bread pan. For a good combination of sourness and leavening, proof the loaf for the first hour at room temperature and then at 85° to 90°F (29° to 32°C) in a proofing box.

BAKING Place the pan with its shaped, proofed loaf in a cool oven, then turn the temperature to 375°F (190°C) and bake for 70 minutes. When the loaf is baked, remove it from the pan and let cool on a wire rack for at least 15 to 20 minutes before slicing.

Cranberry-Nut Sourdough

The choice of nuts in this bread is yours: we've tried both almonds and walnuts. The mix of either with cranberries is a good one. MAKES TWO 1½-POUND (680 G) LOAVES

2 cups (480 ml) culture from the
Culture Proof (page 31)
1¼ cups (300 ml) water
2 tablespoons sugar
1½ teaspoons salt

½ cup (60 g) sweetened dried
cranberries
½ cup (50 g) chopped nuts
4¾ cups (670 g) unbleached
all-purpose flour

DOUGH PROOF Pour the culture into a mixing bowl. Add the water, sugar, salt, cranberries, and nuts and mix well. Add the flour a cup (140 g) at a time until the dough is too stiff to mix by hand. Turn out onto a floured board and knead in the remaining flour until the dough is smooth and satiny.

Proof the dough overnight (8 to 12 hours) at room temperature, about 70°F (21°C), in a large bowl covered with plastic wrap. During this time, the dough should double in size. After the proof, use a spatula to gently ease the dough out onto a floured board. Allow the dough to rest for 30 minutes. If marked flattening occurs during this time, knead in additional flour before shaping.

LOAF PROOF After the 30-minute rest, divide the dough in two and shape it. Take one half of the dough and flatten it slightly, then lift a portion from the periphery and pull it toward the center. Continue this around the dough mass to form a rough ball (see page 34), then pat and pull into the loaf shape you desire. Repeat with the other half of the dough. Place the shaped loaves in bread pans or on a baking sheet and proof for 2 to 4 hours, until they reach nearly to the top of the pans or double in bulk. For a good combination of sourness and leavening, proof the loaves for the first hour at room temperature and then at 85° to 90°F (29° to 32°C) in a proofing box.

BAKING Place the pans or baking sheet with the shaped loaves in a cool oven, then turn the temperature to 375°F (190°C) and bake for 70 minutes. When the loaves are baked, remove them from the pan and let cool on a wire rack for at least 15 to 20 minutes before slicing.

Cranberry-Blueberry Rye

If you are so fortunate as to have them, fresh blueberries or huckleberries are even better here than frozen. The blueberries and cranberries, along with a light touch of rye, make for a fabulous sourdough. MAKES TWO 1½-POUND (680 G) LOAVES

2 cups (480 ml) culture from the Culture Proof (page 31)
1¼ cups (300 ml) water
1½ teaspoons salt
½ cup (60 g) sweetened dried cranberries

½ cup (75 g) frozen blueberries or huckleberries
2 cups (220 g) light rye flour
2¾ cups (385 g) unbleached all-purpose flour

DOUGH PROOF Pour the culture into a mixing bowl. Add the water, salt, cranberries, and blueberries to the culture and mix well. Add the rye flour and mix well. Add the all-purpose flour a cup (140 g) at a time until the dough is too stiff to mix by hand. Turn out onto a floured board and knead in the remaining flour until the dough is smooth and satiny.

Proof the dough overnight (8 to 12 hours) at room temperature, about 70°F (21°C), in a large bowl covered with plastic wrap. During this time, the dough should double in size. After the proof, use a spatula to gently ease the dough out onto a floured board. Allow the dough to rest for 30 minutes. If marked flattening occurs during this time, knead in additional flour before shaping.

LOAF PROOF After the 30-minute rest, divide the dough in two. Flatten each half slightly, then lift a portion from the periphery and pull it toward the center. Continue this around the dough mass to form a rough ball (see page 34), then pat and pull into the loaf shape you desire. Place the shaped loaves, seam side down, on a baking sheet or in bread pans and proof for 2 to 4 hours, until they double in bulk or reach nearly to the tops of the bread pans. For a good combination of sourness and leavening, proof the loaves for the first hour at room temperature and then at 85° to 90°F (29° to 32°C) in a proofing box.

BAKING Place the pans or baking sheet with the shaped, proofed loaves in a cool oven, then turn the temperature to 375°F (190°C) and bake for 70 minutes. When the loaves are baked, remove them from the pan and let cool on a wire rack for at least 15 to 20 minutes before slicing.

La Cloche Sourdough

In his book The Bread Builders: Hearth Loaves and Masonry Ovens *Daniel Wing has nothing but praise for the bread baking-device called La Cloche. Because Wing is a leading advocate of masonry ovens, his endorsement is worth investigating. La Cloche is somewhat analogous to a home bread machine in that, as with the bread machine, you can only bake one loaf at a time. It is a heavy stoneware baking dish made in two styles, one oval for hearth breads and the other oblong for French or Italian type loaves; you may use either for this recipe. Both styles are equipped with lids. They are a little pricey but they do a terrific job.* MAKES ONE FABULOUS 2^1/$_8$-POUND (1010 G) FRENCH LOAF

1 cup (240 ml) culture from the Culture Proof (page 31)	2 teaspoons salt
1^1/$_2$ cups (360 ml) water	4^1/$_4$ cups (595 g) unbleached all-purpose flour

DOUGH PROOF Pour the culture into a mixing bowl. Add the water and salt to the culture and mix well. Add the flour a cup (140 g) at a time until the dough is too stiff to mix by hand. Turn out onto a floured board and knead in the remaining flour until the dough is smooth and satiny.

Proof the dough overnight (8 to 12 hours) at room temperature, about 70°F (21°C), in a large bowl covered with plastic wrap. During this time, the dough should double in size. After the proof, use a spatula to gently ease the dough out onto a floured board. Allow the dough to rest for 30 minutes. If marked flattening occurs during this time, knead in additional flour before shaping.

LOAF PROOF After the 30-minute rest, shape the dough. Flatten it slightly, then lift a portion from the periphery and pull it toward the center. Continue this around the dough mass to form a rough ball (see page 34), then pat and pull into a French loaf shape about 14 inches (35 cm) long. Carefully place the loaf in the La Cloche and cover with the lid. Proof for 2 to 4 hours, until it doubles in bulk, the first hour at room temperature and then at 85° to 90°F (29° to 32°C) in a proofing box.

BAKING Bake in a preheated oven at 500°F (260°C) with the lid in place. After 30 minutes, reduce the heat to 400°F (200°C), remove the lid, and continue baking for 15 minutes, or until the crust is brown. Remove the loaf from the dish and let cool on a wire rack for at least 15 to 20 minutes before slicing.

Braided Egg Bread

We enjoy making braided bread, and the finished product is attractive. Start the braid at one end and work to the other end, or, to make dough handling easier, you can start in the middle and braid in both directions. MAKES TWO 1^1/$_2$-POUND (680 G) LOAVES

2 cups (480 ml) culture from
   the Culture Proof (page 31)
2 tablespoons (30 g) butter
1 cup (240 ml) milk
2 teaspoons salt
2 tablespoons sugar
2 eggs, beaten
6 cups (840 g) unbleached
   all-purpose flour

GLAZE
1 egg, beaten
Sesame seeds

DOUGH PROOF Pour the culture into a large mixing bowl. Melt the butter, then add the milk to warm. Add the salt and sugar and stir until dissolved. Add this mixture to the culture and mix well, then add the eggs and mix to combine. Add the flour a cup (140 g) at a time until the dough is too stiff to mix by hand. Turn out onto a floured board and knead in the remaining flour until the dough is smooth and satiny.

Proof the dough overnight (8 to 12 hours) at room temperature, about 70°F (21°C), in a large bowl covered with plastic wrap. During this time, the dough should double in size. After the proof, use a spatula to gently ease the dough out onto a floured board. Allow the dough to rest for 30 minutes. If marked flattening occurs during this time, knead in additional flour before shaping.

LOAF PROOF Divide the rested dough in half and form 2 balls. Divide each ball into 3 equal portions and roll each to form a rope about 18 inches (45 cm) long and ^{1}/$_2$ to 1 inch (1.5 to 2.5 cm) in diameter. Alternatively, form each ball into a roll 3 inches (8 cm) in diameter. Roll out until ^{1}/$_2$ inch (1.5 cm) thick and 9 inches (23 cm) wide. With a pizza cutter, cut 6 strips lengthwise, each 1^1/$_2$ inches (4 cm) wide. Fold over each strip to make a rounder strip and pinch the seams together.

Using 3 strands for each braided loaf, lay one strand on a work surface. Cross the other two strands over it in the middle. Starting at the center and working toward one end, alternately cross the outside strands over the one in the center. As you work,

continued

gently pull to taper the ends. When you reach the end, pinch the ends together to finish. Then, starting at the center, braid toward the other end, pinching the ends together to finish. Repeat with the other 3 strands of dough to form a second loaf.

Place the braided loaves on a baking sheet and proof for 2 to 4 hours until the loaves double in bulk. For a good combination of sourness and leavening, proof the loaves for the first hour at room temperature and then at 85° to 90°F (29° to 32°C) in a proofing box.

BAKING Just before baking, brush the surface of the dough with the beaten egg and sprinkle with sesame seeds. Place the sheet in a cool oven, then turn the temperature to 375°F (190°C) and bake for 45 to 50 minutes. When the loaves are baked, remove them from the baking sheet and let cool on a wire rack for at least 15 to 20 minutes before slicing.

Challah

This is the classic Jewish Sabbath egg- and butter-enriched bread formed into a single giant braid. MAKES ONE LARGE 3-POUND (1350 G) LOAF

4 cups (960 ml) culture from the
Culture Proof (page 31)
3 tablespoons (45 g) butter
1 cup (240 ml) milk
2 teaspoons salt
3 tablespoons (45 g) sugar
2 eggs, beaten
6 cups (840 g) unbleached
all-purpose flour

GLAZE
1 egg, beaten
1 tablespoon sesame seeds

DOUGH PROOF Pour the culture into a large mixing bowl. Melt the butter, then add the milk to warm. Add the salt and sugar and stir until dissolved, then stir in the eggs. Add this mixture to the culture and mix well. Add the flour a cup (140 g) at a time until the dough is too stiff to mix by hand. Turn out onto a floured board and knead in the remaining flour until the dough is smooth and satiny.

Proof the dough overnight (8 to 12 hours) at room temperature, about 70°F (21°C), in a large bowl covered with plastic wrap. During this time, the dough should double in size. After the proof, use a spatula to gently ease the dough out onto a floured board.

Allow the dough to rest for 30 minutes. If marked flattening occurs during this time, knead in additional flour before shaping.

LOAF PROOF Divide the rested dough into 4 balls of equal size. Roll each ball into a rope 18 to 20 inches (45 to 50 cm) long and 1 inch (2.5 cm) in diameter. Pinch the 4 ropes together at one end and braid by bringing the rope on the right over the one next to it, under the third one and over the last one. Repeat, always starting with the rope on the right, until the braid is complete. Pinch the ends together to finish.

Place the braided loaf on a baking sheet and proof for 2 to 4 hours, until it doubles in bulk. Proof for the first hour at room temperature and then at 85° to 90°F (29° to 32°C) in a proofing box.

continued

Challa, continued

BAKING Just before baking, brush the loaf with the beaten egg and sprinkle with sesame seeds. Place the baking sheet in a cool oven, then turn the temperature to 375°F (190°C) and bake for 45 to 50 minutes. When the loaf is baked, remove it from the pan and let cool on a wire rack for at least 15 to 20 minutes before slicing.

Malt Beer Bread

When making this loaf, you can experiment with different beers. We have often used imported malt beers from Germany and Scandinavia to complement the rye flavor; many local beers being produced in microbreweries are just as good. MAKES ONE 1½-POUND (680 G) LOAF

1 cup (240 ml) culture from the
   Culture Proof (page 31)
2 tablespoons (30 g) melted butter
1 teaspoon salt
1 tablespoon sugar

1 cup (240 ml) malt beer
1¾ cups (200 g) rye flour
1¾ cups (245 g) unbleached
   all-purpose flour

DOUGH PROOF Pour the culture into a mixing bowl. In a separate bowl, combine the butter, salt, sugar, and beer and stir until the salt and sugar are dissolved. Add this mixture to the culture and mix well. Mix in the rye flour. Add the all-purpose flour a cup (140 g) at a time until the dough becomes too stiff to mix by hand. Turn out onto a floured board and knead in the remaining flour until the dough is smooth and satiny.

Or mix and knead all of the ingredients for a maximum of 25 minutes in a bread machine or other mixer (see page 152).

Proof the dough overnight (8 to 12 hours) at room temperature, about 70°F (21°C), in a large bowl covered with plastic wrap (or leave in the machine pan, removed from the machine, securing the plastic wrap with a rubber band). During this time, the dough should double in size in the covered bowl, or rise to the top of the machine pan. After the proof, use a spatula to gently ease the dough out onto a floured board. Allow the dough to rest for 30 minutes. If marked flattening occurs during this time, knead in additional flour before shaping.

LOAF PROOF After the 30-minute rest, shape the dough. Flatten it slightly, then lift a portion from the periphery and pull it toward the center. Continue this around the dough mass to form a rough ball (see page 34), then pat and pull into the loaf shape you desire.

Place the shaped loaf in a bread pan or on a baking sheet and proof for 2 to 4 hours, until it reaches nearly to the top of the pan or doubles in bulk. Proof for the first hour at room temperature and then at 85° to 90°F (29° to 32°C).

continued

Malt Beer Bread, *continued*

BAKING Place the bread pan or baking sheet with its shaped, proofed loaf in a cool oven, then turn the temperature to 375°F (190°C) and bake for 70 minutes. Or transfer the loaf to a preheated baking stone in a 450°F (230°C) oven and bake for 40 minutes. When the loaf is baked, remove it from the pan and let cool on a wire rack for at least 15 to 20 minutes before slicing.

Baguettes

This chewy French loaf should be made as long as possible: the recipe says 18 inches (45 cm), but if your oven is bigger and you have a bigger baking sheet, stretch the roll to fit. There are several baguette molds available that help form the characteristic shape of this loaf; Wilton makes one made of aluminum that is 17 by 9 inches (43 by 23 cm) and contains spaces for three baguettes. It is a good idea to put a baking sheet under this mold to make it easier to maneuver in and out of the oven. MAKES THREE 2-POUND (680 G) LOAVES

4 cups (960 ml) culture from the
    Culture Proof (page 31)
2 tablespoons (30 g) butter
1 cup (240 ml) milk
2 teaspoons salt

2 tablespoons sugar
6 cups (840 g) unbleached
    all-purpose flour
2 eggs, beaten

DOUGH PROOF Pour the culture into a large mixing bowl. Melt the butter over moderate heat and add the milk to the butter to warm it. Add the salt and sugar and stir until dissolved. Add this mixture to the culture and mix well. Add the flour a cup (140 g) at a time until the dough is too stiff to mix by hand. Turn out onto a floured board and knead in the remaining flour until the dough is smooth and satiny.

Proof the dough overnight (8 to 12 hours) at room temperature, about 70°F (21°C), in a large bowl covered with plastic wrap. During this time, the dough should double in size. After the proof, use a spatula to gently ease the dough out onto a floured board. Allow the dough to rest for 30 minutes. If marked flattening occurs during this time, knead in additional flour before shaping.

LOAF PROOF To shape, divide the rested dough into thirds and form 3 balls. Use a rolling pin to form a rectangle from each ball. Roll each rectangle from the long side to form an elongated loaf about 18 inches (45 cm) long and 1½ inches (4 cm) in diameter.

Place the loaves, seam side down, on a baking sheet and proof for 2 to 4 hours, until they double in bulk. Proof for the first hour at room temperature and then at 85° to 90°F (29° to 32°C) in a proofing box.

continued

BAKING Just before putting the loaves in the oven, slash the surface of the dough several times with a razor blade, then brush the loaves with the beaten egg. Place the pan with its shaped, proofed loaves in a cool oven, then turn the temperature to 375°F (190°C) and bake for 70 minutes. Or transfer the loaves to a preheated baking stone in a 450°F (230°C) oven and bake for 40 minutes. When the loaves are baked, remove them from the pan and let cool on a wire rack for at least 15 to 20 minutes before slicing.

Bread Ring

Bread rings and braided pastries are common in the Middle East; this recipe produces a fine, light, and delicious loaf. When you want to experiment, replace one cup (140 g) of white flour with a cup (130 g) of Kamut or spelt. MAKES ONE 1½-POUND (680 G) RING

2 cups (480 ml) culture from the
  Culture Proof (page 31)
1 teaspoon salt
1 tablespoon sugar
½ cup (120 ml) water

2 tablespoons oil
3 cups (420 g) unbleached
  all-purpose flour
Sesame seeds

DOUGH PROOF Pour the culture into a mixing bowl. Add the salt, sugar, water, and oil and stir to mix. Add the flour a cup (140 g) at a time until the dough is too stiff to mix by hand. Turn out onto a floured board and knead in the remaining flour until the dough is smooth and satiny.

Proof the dough overnight (8 to 12 hours) at room temperature, about 70°F (21°C), in a large bowl covered with plastic wrap. During this time, the dough should double in size. After the proof, use a spatula to gently ease the dough out onto a floured board. Allow the dough to rest for 30 minutes. If marked flattening occurs during this time, knead in additional flour before shaping.

LOAF PROOF Using your hands or a rolling pin, flatten the rested dough into a large oval, then roll it up with your hands into a tight rope. Continue rolling the rope back and forth until it is 20 to 24 inches (50 to 60 cm) long. Form the dough into a ring by joining the ends of the rope and pinching them together.

Place the ring on a baking sheet and proof for 2 to 4 hours, until it doubles in bulk. Proof for the first hour at room temperature and then at 85° to 90°F (29° to 32°C) in a proofing box.

BAKING Just before baking, brush the top of the ring with water and sprinkle with sesame seeds. Bake in a preheated oven at 375°F (190°C) for 35 to 40 minutes. When the ring is baked, remove it to a wire rack to cool for at least 15 to 20 minutes before slicing.

Cheese Bread

This is a pleasing, cheese-filled variation on traditional Middle Eastern flatbreads. MAKES
ONE 1½-POUND (680 G) LOAF

2 cups (480 ml) culture from the
  Culture Proof (page 31)
1 teaspoon salt
2 teaspoons sugar
1 cup (240 ml) water
2 tablespoons oil

3½ cups (490 g) unbleached
  all-purpose flour
8 ounces (225 g) cream cheese,
  softened
1 egg, beaten
Sesame seeds

DOUGH PROOF In a mixing bowl, combine the culture, salt, sugar, water, and oil
and mix well. Add the flour a cup (140 g) at a time until the dough becomes too stiff
to mix by hand. Turn out onto a floured board and knead in the remaining flour
until the dough is smooth and satiny.

Or mix and knead all of the ingredients for a maximum of 25 minutes in a bread
machine or other mixer (see page 152).

Proof the dough overnight (8 to 12 hours) at room temperature, about 70°F (21°C),
in a large bowl covered with plastic wrap (or leave in the machine pan, removed
from the machine, securing the plastic wrap with a rubber band). During this time,
the dough should double in size in the covered bowl, or rise to the top of the machine
pan. After the proof, use a spatula to gently ease the dough out onto a floured board.
Allow the dough to rest for 30 minutes. If marked flattening occurs during this time,
knead in additional flour before shaping.

LOAF PROOF Using your hands or a rolling pin, flatten the rested dough into a
rectangle ½ inch (1.5 cm) thick. Gently spread the cream cheese over the dough rectangle, making sure not to tear the dough and leaving 1 inch (2.5 cm) of margin clear.
Roll the dough up from the long side and pinch the edges and ends to seal, forming
an elongated oval loaf.

Place the loaf on a baking sheet and proof for 2 to 4 hours, until it doubles in bulk.
Proof for the first hour at room temperature and then at 85° to 90°F (29° to 32°C)
in a proofing box.

BAKING Just before baking, brush the top of the loaf with the beaten egg and sprinkle with sesame seeds. Put the baking sheet with its shaped loaf in a cool oven, then turn the temperature to 375°F (190°C) and bake for 65 to 70 minutes. When the loaf is baked, remove it from the pan and let cool on a wire rack for at least 15 to 20 minutes before slicing.

Cheese-Onion Bread

Fresh chopped onions added to this cheese bread yields a truly delicious loaf. The onion adds liquid, which sometimes requires additional flour. Test the loaf with a digital thermometer when it is removed from the oven: the center should be 190°F (88°C). If serving after the loaf has fully cooled, toast slices to recapture the "right out of the oven" aroma. This recipe can also be used for braided loaves. MAKES TWO 1¹/₂-POUND (680 G) LOAVES

2 cups (480 ml) culture from the
   Culture Proof (page 31)
2 tablespoons (30 g) butter
1 cup (240 ml) milk
2 teaspoons salt

2 tablespoons sugar
2 cups (240 g) grated cheddar cheese
1 cup (150 g) finely chopped onions
6 cups (840 g) unbleached
   all-purpose flour

DOUGH PROOF Pour the culture into a large mixing bowl. Melt the butter and add the milk to warm. Add the salt, sugar, cheese, and onions and stir to combine. Add this mixture to the culture and mix well. Add the flour a cup (140 g) at a time until the dough is too stiff to mix by hand. Turn out onto a floured board and knead in the remaining flour until the dough is smooth and satiny.

Proof the dough overnight (8 to 12 hours) at room temperature, about 70°F (21°C), in a large bowl covered with plastic wrap. During this time, the dough should double in size in the covered bowl. After the proof, use a spatula to gently ease the dough out onto a floured board. Allow the dough to rest for 30 minutes. If marked flattening occurs during this time, knead in additional flour before shaping.

LOAF PROOF Divide the rested dough in half and form 2 balls. Pat each ball into an oval 1 inch (2.5 cm) thick and form loaves by rolling the ovals from the long side, then pinching the dough together to form a seam.

Place the loaves, seam side down, on a baking sheet or in pans and proof for 2 to 4 hours or longer, until they double in bulk or rise 1 to 2 inches (2.5 to 5 cm) above the tops of the pans. This is a moist dough and may take longer to rise. Proof for the first hour at room temperature and then at 85° to 90°F (29° to 32°C) in a proofing box.

BAKING Place the pans with their shaped, proofed loaves in a cool oven, then turn the temperature to 375°F (190°C) and bake for 70 minutes. When the loaves are baked, remove them from the pan and let cool on a wire rack for at least 15 to 20 minutes before slicing.

Onion Bread

Onions and rye flour provide a pleasing flavor combination. This recipe uses chopped onions lightly sautéed in olive oil. Raw chopped onions work well, and dried onion can also be used. (Note that raw onions will increase the liquid in the loaf as it bakes, possibly necessitating extra flour.) MAKES TWO 1¹/₂-POUND (680 G) LOAVES

2 cups (480 ml) culture from the
    Culture Proof (page 31)
1 cup (150 g) chopped onions
1 tablespoon olive oil
2 tablespoons (30 g) butter

¹/₂ cup (120 ml) water
2 teaspoons salt
3 cups (340 g) rye flour
3 cups (420 g) unbleached
    all-purpose flour

DOUGH PROOF Pour the culture into a large mixing bowl. Over moderate heat, sauté the onions in the olive oil until they are soft but not browned. In a separate pan, melt the butter and add the water to the butter. Add the salt to the butter and water mixture and stir until dissolved, then stir in the onions and oil. Scrape this mixture into the culture and mix well, then add the rye flour and mix well. Add the all-purpose flour 1 cup (140 g) at a time until the dough is too stiff to mix by hand. Turn out onto a floured board and knead in the remaining flour until the dough is smooth and satiny.

Proof the dough overnight (8 to 12 hours) at room temperature, about 70°F (21°C), in a large bowl covered with plastic wrap. During this time, the dough should double in size in the covered bowl. After the proof, use a spatula to gently ease the dough out onto a floured board. Allow the dough to rest for 30 minutes. If marked flattening occurs during this time, knead in additional flour before shaping.

LOAF PROOF Divide the rested dough in half and form 2 balls, then shape the balls into 2 elongated loaves. Place the loaves, seam side down, in bread pans or on a baking sheet and proof for 2 to 4 hours, until the loaves reach nearly to the tops of the pans or double in bulk. Proof for the first hour at room temperature and then at 85° to 90°F (29° to 32°C) in a proofing box.

BAKING Just before putting the loaves in the oven, slash the surface of the dough several times with a razor blade. Place the pans in a cool oven, then turn the temperature to 375°F (190°C) and bake for 70 minutes. When the loaves are baked, remove them from the pan and let cool on a wire rack for at least 15 to 20 minutes before slicing.

Onion-Olive Bread

This delicious filled bread is modeled on breads baked in Greece and Cyprus. MAKES ONE
2-POUND (900 G) LOAF

1 onion, finely chopped
1 tablespoon olive oil, plus more
   for brushing
1 cup (180 g) chopped black olives
2 cups (480 ml) culture from the
   Culture Proof (page 31)

1 teaspoon salt
2¹/₂ cups (350 g) unbleached
   all-purpose flour

DOUGH PROOF Sauté the onion in the 1 tablespoon olive oil until soft and just trans-
lucent. Stir the olives into the onions, set aside to cool, and refrigerate until ready to use.

Pour the culture into a mixing bowl. Add the salt to the culture and mix well.
Add the flour a cup (140 g) at a time until the dough is too stiff to mix by hand. Turn
out onto a floured board and knead in the remaining flour until the dough is smooth
and satiny.

Proof the dough overnight (8 to 12 hours) at room temperature, about 70°F
(21°C), in a large bowl covered with plastic wrap. During this time, the dough
should double in size. After the proof, use a spatula to gently ease the dough out
onto a floured board. Allow the dough to rest for 30 minutes. If marked flattening
occurs during this time, knead in additional flour before shaping.

LOAF PROOF Using your hands or a rolling pin, flatten the rested dough into a
rectangle about ¹/₂ inch (1.5 cm) thick. Spread the onion and olive mixture over the
surface of the dough rectangle, leaving 1 inch (2.5 cm) clear at the edges. Roll the
rectangle up from the long side into a loaf and pinch the edges to seal.

Place the shaped loaf, seam side down, on a baking sheet and proof for 2 to 4 hours,
until it doubles in bulk. Proof the loaf for the first hour at room temperature and
then at 85° to 90°F (29° to 32°C) in a proofing box.

BAKING Just before baking, make several diagonal slashes in the dough with a razor
blade and brush the top of the loaf with olive oil. Place the baking sheet with its shaped
loaf in a cool oven, then turn the temperature to 375°F (190°C) and bake for 65 to
70 minutes. When the loaf is baked, remove it from the pan and let cool on a wire rack
for at least 15 to 20 minutes before slicing.

Potato Bread

The addition of mashed potato provides a distinctive flavor and texture to this hearty white bread. Many sourdough bakers once fed their starters with boiled potatoes, but the addition here is for flavor. (Naturally, we use our homegrown Idaho spuds!) MAKES ONE 1½-POUND (680 G) LOAF

1 cup (240 ml) culture from the
   Culture Proof (page 31)
1 tablespoon (15 g) butter
1 cup (240 ml) milk
1 teaspoon salt

1 medium baking potato, peeled,
   boiled, and mashed
3½ cups (490 g) unbleached
   all-purpose flour

DOUGH PROOF Pour the culture into a mixing bowl. Melt the butter over moderate heat and add the milk to warm. Add the salt and potato and stir well. Stir this mixture into the culture. Add the flour a cup (140 g) at a time until the dough is too stiff to mix by hand. Turn out onto a floured board and knead in the remaining flour until the dough is smooth and satiny.

Or mix and knead all of the ingredients for a maximum of 25 minutes in a bread machine or other mixer (see page 152).

Proof the dough overnight (8 to 12 hours) at room temperature, about 70°F (21°C), in a large bowl covered with plastic wrap (or leave in the machine pan, removed from the machine, securing the plastic wrap with a rubber band). During this time, the dough should double in size in the covered bowl, or rise to the top of the machine pan. After the proof, use a spatula to gently ease the dough out onto a floured board. Allow the dough to rest for 30 minutes. If marked flattening occurs during this time, knead in additional flour before shaping.

LOAF PROOF Flatten the rested dough slightly, then lift a portion from the periphery and pull it toward the center. Continue this around the dough mass to form a rough ball (see page 34), then pat and pull into the loaf shape you desire. Place the shaped loaf, seam side down, on a baking sheet or in a bread pan and proof for 2 to 4 hours, until it doubles in bulk or reaches nearly to the top of the bread pan. Proof the loaf for the first hour at room temperature and then at 85° to 90°F (29° to 32°C) in a proofing box.

continued

BAKING Place the pan with its shaped, proofed loaf in a cool oven, then turn the temperature to 375°F (190°C) and bake for 70 minutes. Or transfer the loaf to a preheated baking stone in a 450°F (230°C) oven and bake for 40 minutes. When the loaf is baked, remove it from the pan and let cool on a wire rack for at least 15 to 20 minutes before slicing.

Rosemary Bread

This Italian bread is baked especially for Easter. Fresh rosemary can be heated in olive oil to flavor the oil, which is used to bake the bread (the rosemary is discarded). This recipe, however, uses dried rosemary added directly to the dough mixture. **MAKES ONE 1½-POUND (680 G) LOAF**

2 cups (480 ml) culture from the
Culture Proof (page 31)
½ cup (120 ml) milk
¼ cup (60 ml) olive oil
1 teaspoon salt
1 tablespoon sugar

1 teaspoon ground dried rosemary
½ cup (80 g) raisins
3 eggs, beaten
3 cups (420 g) unbleached
all-purpose flour

DOUGH PROOF Pour the culture into a mixing bowl. Add the milk, olive oil, salt, sugar, rosemary, raisins, and 2 of the beaten eggs and mix well. Add the flour a cup (140 g) at a time until the dough becomes too stiff to mix by hand. Turn out onto a floured board and knead in the remaining flour until the dough is smooth and satiny.

Proof the dough overnight (8 to 12 hours) at room temperature, about 70°F (21°C), in a large bowl covered with plastic wrap. During this time, the dough should double in size. After the proof, use a spatula to gently ease the dough out onto a floured board. Allow the dough to rest for 30 minutes. If marked flattening occurs during this time, knead in additional flour before shaping.

LOAF PROOF To shape the rested dough, flatten it slightly, then lift a portion from the periphery and pull it toward the center. Continue this around the dough mass to form a rough ball (see page 34), then pat and pull into an oval or round loaf. Place on a baking sheet or in a bread pan and proof for 2 to 4 hours, until it doubles in bulk or reaches nearly to the top of the bread pan. Proof for the first hour at room temperature and then at 85° to 90°F (30° to 32°C) in a proofing box.

BAKING Just before baking, make crisscross slashes in the crust and brush the dough with the remaining beaten egg. Put the pan or baking sheet with its shaped, proofed loaf in a cool oven, then turn the temperature to 375°F (190°C) and bake for 65 minutes. When the loaf is baked, remove it from the pan and let cool on a wire rack for at least 15 to 20 minutes before slicing.

Graham and Cracked Wheat Bread

Cracked wheat is produced by cutting the grain instead of grinding it. It can be used raw, as in this recipe, or cooked. If cooked, it is usually presoaked for several hours and then simmered for about one hour in two cups (240 ml) of water for every cup (120 g) of cracked grain. MAKES TWO 1½-POUND (680 G) LOAVES

2 cups (480 ml) culture from the
   Culture Proof (page 31)
2 tablespoons (30 g) butter
1 cup (240 ml) milk
2 teaspoons salt
½ cup (120 ml) molasses

2 tablespoons sugar
¼ cup (30 g) cracked wheat
1½ cups (195 g) graham flour
5 cups (700 g) unbleached
   all-purpose flour

DOUGH PROOF Pour the culture into a large mixing bowl. Melt the butter over moderate heat and add the milk to warm. Add the salt, molasses, and sugar and stir to combine. Add this mixture to the culture and mix well, then add the cracked wheat and graham flour and mix well. Add the all-purpose flour a cup (140 g) at a time until the dough is too stiff to mix by hand. Turn out onto a floured board and knead in the remaining flour until the dough is smooth and satiny.

Proof the dough overnight (8 to 12 hours) at room temperature, about 70°F (21°C), in a large bowl covered with plastic wrap. During this time, the dough should double in size. After the proof, use a spatula to gently ease the dough out onto a floured board. Allow the dough to rest for 30 minutes. If marked flattening occurs during this time, knead in additional flour before shaping.

LOAF PROOF Divide the rested dough in half and shape it into 2 balls and then into 2 loaves. Place, seam side down, on a baking sheet or in bread pans and proof for 2 to 4 hours, until the loaves have doubled in bulk or nearly reached the tops of the bread pans. Proof for the first hour at room temperature and then at 85° to 90°F (29° to 32°C) in a proofing box.

BAKING Place the pans with the shaped, proofed loaves in a cool oven, then turn the temperature to 375°F (190°C) and bake for 65 to 70 minutes. When the loaves are baked, remove them from the pan and let cool on a wire rack for at least 15 to 20 minutes before slicing.

Barm Brack

"Barm" means homemade yeast, and this recipe, which is popular in southern Ireland, is great for sourdough. Note that this bread does not require a dough proof. MAKES TWO 1¹/₂-POUND (680 G) LOAVES

2 cups (480 ml) culture from the
   Culture Proof (page 31)
1 cup (240 g) butter
1 cup (240 ml) milk
2 teaspoons salt
1 cup (215 g) brown sugar

4 eggs, beaten
¹/₂ teaspoon ground nutmeg
1 tablespoon caraway seed
6 cups (840 g) unbleached
   all-purpose flour

Pour the culture into a mixing bowl. Melt the butter over moderate heat and add the milk to warm. Stir in the salt, brown sugar, eggs, nutmeg, and caraway seed. Add this mixture to the culture and mix well. Add the flour a cup (140 g) at a time until the dough is too stiff to mix by hand. Turn out onto a floured board and knead in the remaining flour until the dough is smooth and satiny.

LOAF PROOF Divide the dough in half. Shape each half into a ball: flatten it slightly, then lift a portion from the periphery and pull it toward the center. Continue this around the dough mass to form a rough ball (see page 34), then pat and pull into a loaf. Place the shaped loaves, seam side down, on a baking sheet or in bread pans and proof for 2 to 4 hours, until the loaves have doubled in bulk or nearly reached the tops of the pans. Proof for the first hour at room temperature and then at 85° to 90°F (29° to 32°C) in a proofing box.

BAKING Place the pans with the shaped, proofed loaves in a cool oven, then turn the temperature to 375°F (190°C) and bake for 70 minutes. Let the loaves cool in the pans.

Oatmeal Bread

This recipe produces an interesting variation on a standard sourdough loaf. It is somewhat rougher in texture, but it rises well. You may use either rolled oats or steel-cut oats; don't use instant oats. MAKES TWO 1¹/₂-POUND (680 G) LOAVES

2 cups (480 ml) culture from the
   Culture Proof (page 31)
¹/₂ cup (120 ml) milk
1 cup (240 ml) water
1 teaspoon salt

2 tablespoons brown sugar
2 cups (230 g) rolled oats, or 2 cups
   (320 g) steel-cut oats
4 cups (560 g) unbleached
   all-purpose flour

DOUGH PROOF Pour the culture into a large mixing bowl. Add the milk, water, salt, sugar, and oats and mix well. Add the flour a cup (140 g) at a time until the dough becomes too stiff to mix by hand. Turn out onto a floured board and knead in the remaining flour until the dough is smooth and satiny.

Proof the dough overnight (8 to 12 hours) at room temperature, about 70°F (21°C), in a large bowl covered with plastic wrap. During this time, the dough should double in size. After the proof, use a spatula to gently ease the dough out onto a floured board. Allow the dough to rest for 30 minutes. If marked flattening occurs during this time, knead in additional flour before shaping.

LOAF PROOF Divide the rested dough in half and shape into 2 balls, and then into loaves. Place the shaped loaves, seam side down, on a baking sheet or in bread pans and proof for 2 to 4 hours, until the loaves have doubled in bulk or nearly reached the tops of the pans. Proof for the first hour at room temperature and then at 85° to 90°F (29° to 32°C) in a proofing box.

BAKING Place the pans or sheet with the shaped, proofed loaves in a cool oven, then turn the temperature to 375°F (190°C) and bake for 70 minutes. Or transfer the loaves to a preheated baking stone in a 450°F (230°C) oven and bake for 40 minutes. When the loaves are baked, remove them from the pan and let cool on a wire rack for at least 15 to 20 minutes before slicing.

Sunflower Bread

In this recipe, sunflower seeds can be used either raw—which we much prefer—or roasted. To roast, place them in a 300°F (150°C) oven for 30 minutes, turning occasionally to prevent scorching. MAKES ONE 1¹/₂-POUND (680 G) LOAF

1 cup (240 ml) culture from the
  Culture Proof (page 31)
1 tablespoon (15 g) butter
1 cup (240 ml) milk
¹/₂ cup (120 ml) water
1 teaspoon salt

¹/₄ cup (60 ml) honey
¹/₂ cup (50 g) sunflower seeds
1¹/₂ cups (210 g) whole wheat flour
2 cups (280 g) unbleached
  all-purpose flour

DOUGH PROOF Pour the culture into a mixing bowl. Melt the butter and add the milk and water to warm. Stir in the salt, honey, and sunflower seeds and add this mixture to the culture; mix well. Add the whole wheat flour, then add the all-purpose flour a cup (140 g) at a time until the dough becomes too stiff to mix by hand. Turn out onto a floured board and knead in the remaining flour until the dough is smooth and satiny.

Or mix and knead all of the ingredients for a maximum of 25 minutes in a bread machine or other mixer (see page 152).

Proof the dough overnight (8 to 12 hours) at room temperature, about 70°F (21°C), in a large bowl covered with plastic wrap (or leave in the machine pan, removed from the machine, securing the plastic wrap with a rubber band). During this time, the dough should double in size in the covered bowl, or rise to the top of the machine pan. After the proof, use a spatula to gently ease the dough out onto a floured board. Allow the dough to rest for 30 minutes. If marked flattening occurs during this time, knead in additional flour before shaping.

LOAF PROOF After the 30-minute rest, shape the dough. Flatten it slightly, then lift a portion from the periphery and pull it toward the center. Continue this around the dough mass to form a rough ball (see page 34), then pat and pull into the loaf shape you desire.

Place the shaped loaf on a baking sheet or in a bread pan and proof for 2 to 4 hours, until it doubles in bulk or rises nearly to the top of the pan. Proof for the first hour at room temperature and then at 85° to 90°F (29° to 32°C) in a proofing box.

continued

BAKING Place the pan with its shaped, proofed loaf in a cool oven, then turn the temperature to 375°F (190°C) and bake for 70 minutes. Or transfer the loaf to a pre-heated baking stone in a 450°F (230°C) oven and bake for 40 minutes. When the loaf is baked, remove it from the pan and let cool on a wire rack for at least 15 to 20 minutes before slicing.

Walnut Bread

This recipe calls for chopped walnuts, but other nuts are equally suitable and a mixture is even better. The ginger is essential for an exquisite flavor. MAKES ONE 1½-POUND (680 G) LOAF

1 cup (240 ml) culture from the
    Culture Proof (page 31)
1 tablespoon (15 g) butter
1 cup (240 ml) milk
1 teaspoon salt
¾ cup (75 g) chopped walnuts

½ cup (120 ml) honey
½ teaspoon ground ginger
1½ cups (210 g) whole wheat flour
1½ cups (210 g) unbleached
    all-purpose flour

DOUGH PROOF Pour the culture into a mixing bowl. Melt the butter and add the milk to warm. Stir in the salt, walnuts, honey, and ginger. Add this mixture to the culture and mix well. Add the whole wheat flour and mix well. Add the all-purpose flour a cup (140 g) at a time until the dough becomes too stiff to mix by hand. Turn out onto a floured board and knead in the remaining flour until the dough is smooth and satiny.

Or mix and knead all of the ingredients for a maximum of 25 minutes in a bread machine or other mixer (see page 152).

Proof the dough overnight (8 to 12 hours) at room temperature, about 70°F (21°C), in a large bowl covered with plastic wrap (or leave in the machine pan, removed from the machine, securing the plastic wrap with a rubber band). During this time, the dough should double in size in the covered bowl, or rise to the top of the machine pan. After the proof, use a spatula to gently ease the dough out onto a floured board. Allow the dough to rest for 30 minutes. If marked flattening occurs during this time, knead in additional flour before shaping.

LOAF PROOF After the 30-minute rest, shape the dough. Flatten it slightly, then lift a portion from the periphery and pull it toward the center. Continue this around the dough mass to form a rough ball (see page 34), then pat and pull into the loaf shape you desire. Place on a baking sheet or in a bread pan and proof for 2 to 4 hours, until the loaf doubles in bulk or rises nearly to the top of the pan. Proof for the first hour at room temperature and then at 85° to 90°F (29° to 32°C) in a proofing box.

BAKING Place the pan with its shaped, proofed loaf in a cool oven, then turn the temperature to 375°F (190°C) and bake for 70 minutes. Or transfer the loaf to a preheated baking stone in a 450°F (230°C) oven and bake for 40 minutes. When the loaf is baked, remove it from the pan and let cool on a wire rack for at least 15 to 20 minutes before slicing.

Herb Bread

This loaf is delightful, with a mixture of thyme, oregano, and basil. MAKES ONE 1¹/₂-POUND
(680 G) LOAF

1 cup (240 ml) culture from the
    Culture Proof (page 31)
1 tablespoon (15 g) butter
1 cup (240 ml) milk
1 teaspoon salt
1 teaspoon sugar

¹/₂ teaspoon dried thyme
¹/₂ teaspoon dried oregano
¹/₂ teaspoon crushed dried basil
3¹/₂ cups (490 g) unbleached
    all-purpose flour

DOUGH PROOF Pour the culture into a mixing bowl. Melt the butter and add the
milk to warm. Stir in the salt, sugar, thyme, oregano, and basil and stir. Add the butter mixture to the culture and mix well. Add the flour a cup (140 g) at a time until the
dough becomes too stiff to mix by hand. Turn out onto a floured board and knead in
the remaining flour until the dough is smooth and satiny.

Or mix and knead all of the ingredients for a maximum of 25 minutes in a bread
machine or other mixer (see page 152).

Proof the dough overnight (8 to 12 hours) at room temperature, about 70°F (21°C),
in a large bowl covered with plastic wrap (or leave in the machine pan, removed
from the machine, securing the plastic wrap with a rubber band). During this time,
the dough should double in size in the covered bowl, or rise to the top of the machine
pan. After the proof, use a spatula to gently ease the dough out onto a floured board.
Allow the dough to rest for 30 minutes. If marked flattening occurs during this time,
knead in additional flour before shaping.

LOAF PROOF After the 30-minute rest, shape the dough. Flatten it slightly, then lift
a portion from the periphery and pull it toward the center. Continue this around the
dough mass to form a rough ball (see page 34), then pat and pull into the loaf shape
you desire. Place on a baking sheet or in a bread pan and proof for 2 to 4 hours, until
it doubles in bulk or rises nearly to the top of the pan. Proof for the first hour at room
temperature and then at 85° to 90°F (29° to 32°C) in a proofing box.

BAKING Place the pan with its shaped, proofed loaf in a cool oven, then turn the temperature to 375°F (190°C) and bake for 70 minutes. Or transfer the loaf to a preheated baking stone in a 450°F (230°C) oven and bake for 40 minutes. When the loaf is baked, remove it from the pan and let cool on a wire rack for at least 15 to 20 minutes before slicing.

Cinnamon-Raisin-Nut Bread

This is an excellent bread for your morning toast. Note that it is a rather heavy dough and may take as long as three hours to rise, so make it well in advance. MAKES TWO 1½-POUND (680 G) LOAVES

4 cups (960 ml) culture from the
    Culture Proof (page 31)
2 tablespoons (30 g) butter
1 cup (240 ml) milk
2 teaspoons salt
2 tablespoons sugar
2 tablespoons ground cinnamon
1 cup (100 g) chopped nuts

1 cup (160 g) raisins
6 cups (840 g) unbleached
    all-purpose flour

FILLING
2 tablespoons ground cinnamon
½ cup (100 g) sugar

DOUGH PROOF Pour the culture into a large mixing bowl. Melt the butter and add the milk to warm it. Stir in the salt, sugar, and cinnamon, then pour this mixture into the culture and mix briefly. Stir in the nuts and raisins. Add the flour a cup (140 g) at a time until the dough is too stiff to mix by hand. Turn out onto a floured board and knead in the remaining flour until the dough is smooth and satiny.

Proof the dough overnight (8 to 12 hours) at room temperature, about 70°F (21°C), in a large bowl covered with plastic wrap. During this time, the dough should double in size. After the proof, use a spatula to gently ease the dough out onto a floured board. Allow the dough to rest for 30 minutes. If marked flattening occurs during this time, knead in additional flour before shaping.

LOAF PROOF Divide the rested dough in half and form it into 2 balls. Roll the balls into rectangles the width of your baking sheet and about ½ inch (1.5 cm) thick. To make the filling, mix the cinnamon with the sugar. Sprinkle half of this mixture onto each rectangle. Roll the rectangles up from the short side to form loaves.

Place the loaves, seam side down, on a baking sheet and proof for 2 to 4 hours, until the loaves double in bulk. Proof for the first hour at room temperature and then at 85° to 90°F (29° to 32°C) in a proofing box.

BAKING Place the pan with its shaped, proofed loaves in a cool oven, then turn the temperature to 375°F (190°C) and bake for 70 minutes. When the loaves are baked, remove them from the pan and let cool on a wire rack for at least 15 to 20 minutes before slicing.

Austrian Christmas Bread

To influence leavening and texture, refer to chapter 3 (pages 31–35) for variations in timing and temperature during the proofing stages. MAKES ONE 1¹/₂-POUND (680 G) LOAF

2 cups (480 ml) culture from the
  Culture Proof (page 31)
¹/₂ cup (120 ml) milk
¹/₂ cup (120 ml) water
2 eggs, beaten
¹/₂ cup (60 g) candied citron

¹/₂ cup (80 g) raisins
1 tablespoon anise seed
1 teaspoon salt
3 tablespoons (45 g) sugar
4 cups (560 g) unbleached
  all-purpose flour

DOUGH PROOF Pour the culture into a mixing bowl. Add the milk, water, eggs, citron, raisins, anise seed, salt, and sugar and mix well. Add the flour a cup (140 g) at a time until the dough becomes too stiff to mix by hand. Turn out onto a floured board and knead in the remaining flour until the dough is smooth and satiny.

Proof the dough overnight (8 to 12 hours) at room temperature, about 70°F (21°C), in a large bowl covered with plastic wrap. During this time, the dough should double in size. After the proof, use a spatula to gently ease the dough out onto a floured board. Allow the dough to rest for 30 minutes. If marked flattening occurs during this time, knead in additional flour before shaping.

LOAF PROOF After the 30-minute rest, shape the dough. Flatten it slightly, then lift a portion from the periphery and pull it toward the center. Continue this around the dough mass to form a rough ball (see page 34), then pat and pull into an oval loaf by flattening the ball into an oval 1¹/₂ inches (4 cm) thick and folding once in half. Pinch the seam together.

Place the shaped loaf, seam side down, on a baking sheet and proof for 2 to 4 hours, until it doubles in bulk. Proof the loaf for the first hour at room temperature and then at 85° to 90°F (29° to 32°C) in a proofing box.

BAKING Place the sheet with its shaped, proofed loaf in a cool oven, then turn the temperature to 375°F (190°C) and bake for 65 to 70 minutes. When the loaf is baked, remove it from the pan and let cool on a wire rack for at least 15 to 20 minutes before slicing.

German Christmas Bread (Stollen)

Sweet, rich yeast breads from Germany are known throughout Europe as "stollen." A mixture of candied fruits can be substituted for the citron. You may top this with a glaze of your choice while it's still warm. **MAKES ONE LARGE 3-POUND (1350 G) STOLLEN**

2 cups (480 ml) culture from the Culture Proof (page 31)	1/2 cup (60 g) candied citron
1/2 cup (120 g) butter	Grated zest of 1 lemon
1 cup (240 ml) milk	1/2 teaspoon ground cinnamon
1 cup (240 ml) water	1/2 teaspoon ground cloves
2 teaspoons salt	1/2 teaspoon ground cardamom
1/2 cup (80 g) raisins	6 cups (840 g) unbleached all-purpose flour
1/2 cup (80 g) currants	

DOUGH PROOF Pour the culture into a large mixing bowl. Melt the butter and add the milk and water to warm. Stir in the salt until dissolved. Add the raisins, currants, citron, lemon zest, cinnamon, cloves, and cardamom to the butter mixture, then pour it into the culture and mix well. Add the flour a cup (140 g) at a time until the dough becomes too stiff to mix by hand. Turn out onto floured board and knead in the remaining flour until the dough is smooth and satiny.

Proof the dough overnight (8 to 12 hours) at room temperature, about 70°F (21°C), in a large bowl covered with plastic wrap. During this time, the dough should double in size. After the proof, use a spatula to gently ease the dough out onto a floured board. Allow the dough to rest for 30 minutes. If marked flattening occurs during this time, knead in additional flour before shaping.

LOAF PROOF After the 30-minute rest, shape the dough. Flatten it slightly, then lift a portion from the periphery and pull it toward the center. Continue this around the dough mass to form a rough ball (see page 34), then pat and pull into an oblong loaf. Place on a baking sheet and proof for 2 to 4 hours, until it doubles in bulk. Proof for the first hour at room temperature and then at 85° to 90°F (29° to 32°C) in a proofing box.

BAKING Place the pan with its shaped, proofed loaf in a cool oven, then turn the temperature to 375°F (190°C) and bake for 70 minutes. When the loaf is baked, remove it from the pan and let cool on a wire rack for at least 15 to 20 minutes before slicing.

Swedish Christmas Bread

The combination of rye, beer, and molasses makes this an unusual Christmas bread. MAKES TWO 1½-POUND (680 G) LOAVES

2 cups (480 ml) culture from the
  Culture Proof (page 31)
2 tablespoons (30 g) butter
2 teaspoons salt
½ cup (120 ml) molasses
1 cup (240 ml) beer

½ cup (60 g) chopped candied
  fruit peel
2 tablespoons anise seed
3 cups (340 g) rye flour
3 cups (420 g) unbleached
  all-purpose flour

DOUGH PROOF Pour the culture into a mixing bowl. Melt the butter, then stir into it the salt, molasses, and beer. Add the candied fruit peel and anise to the mixture, then pour it into the culture and mix well. Add the rye flour and mix well. Add the all-purpose flour a cup (140 g) at a time until the dough becomes too stiff to mix by hand. Turn out onto a floured board and knead in the remaining flour until the dough is smooth and satiny.

Proof the dough overnight (8 to 12 hours) at room temperature, about 70°F (21°C), in a large bowl covered with plastic wrap. During this time, the dough should double in size. After the proof, use a spatula to gently ease the dough out onto a floured board. Allow the dough to rest for 30 minutes. If marked flattening occurs during this time, knead in additional flour before shaping.

LOAF PROOF Shape the rested dough by dividing it in half and forming 2 balls, then pulling and patting the balls into 2 oblong loaves. Place the loaves, seam side down, on a baking sheet and proof for 2 to 4 hours, until the loaves double in bulk. Proof, the first hour at room temperature and then at 85° to 90°F (29° to 32°C) in a proofing box.

BAKING Place the baking sheet with its shaped, proofed loaves in a cool oven, then turn the temperature to 375°F (190°C) and bake for 65 to 70 minutes. When the loaf is baked, remove it from the pan and let cool on a wire rack for at least 15 to 20 minutes before slicing.

No-Knead Sourdoughs

After Jim Lahey's recipe and directions for producing no-knead bread appeared in the *New York Times*, we received a jillion inquiries asking if it is possible to make no-knead sourdoughs. When we looked at Lahey's recipe and focused on his twelve-hour "rest," we immediately felt that lactobacilli fermenting in a sourdough culture for twelve hours would produce a far better flavor than instant yeast or any other commercial yeast, all of which contain very little or no lactobacilli.

Like everyone, we were simply amazed at the results. The crumb was excellent and the aroma and flavor unbelievable. We have repeated the basic recipe (opposite) so many times with identical results that we now use it as the control when we experiment with new recipes containing a great variety of ingredients. We recommend you do the same as you become familiar with the no-knead recipes that follow.

The very nature of the no-knead sourdough process involves some issues of which you should be aware. First, the culture proof is essential. While a fully active culture may look completely adequate to the task, it requires the subsequent six- to ten-hour proof to yield the desired leavening, flavor, and crumb.

Second, the initial mixing of the culture, flour, and other ingredients creates a dry mixture that is difficult to mix adequately. This can be partially resolved by separately combining the dry ingredients and the liquid ingredients including the culture, then combining the dry with the wet. While the final mixing is still somewhat difficult, the consistency is improved; but if it is still too dry—that is, it doesn't hold together— up to $1/2$ cup (120 ml) of water may be added.

Basic No-Knead Sourdough

Almost any sourdough recipe can be converted to no-knead sourdough. This is how we did it the first time. MAKES ONE 1½-POUND (680 G) LOAF

1 cup (240 ml) culture from the
  Culture Proof (page 31)
1 cup (240 ml) water

3½ cups (490 g) unbleached
  all-purpose flour or bread flour
1½ teaspoons salt

DOUGH PROOF In a large mixing bowl, combine the culture and water. Separately, mix together the flour and salt, then add the dry ingredients to the liquid ingredients and mix just until a dry, firm, shaggy dough comes together, adding up to ½ cup (120 ml) more water as needed.

Cover the bowl with plastic wrap and proof for 8 to 12 hours at about 70°F (21°C). (Above 75°F/24°C, the lactobacilli are more active and the dough may become too acidic, inhibiting the wild yeast so it does not leaven as well.) After the 8- to 12-hour fermentation, the dough becomes quite sticky. With a plastic spatula, ease it away from the sides of the bowl onto a lightly floured board. Sprinkle the surface of the dough with additional flour and let it rest for 15 to 30 minutes to relax the gluten.

LOAF PROOF With minimal handling and some additional flour (not more than ¼ cup/30 g), form a loaf and place it in a baking container. The baking container can be almost any small baking dish, such as a bread pan or a covered casserole. Avoid willow baskets, since the sticky dough can be difficult to remove. Proof the dough at room temperature (70°F/21°C) for 3 to 4 hours, until doubled in bulk.

BAKING Place the pan with its shaped, proofed loaf in a cool oven, then turn the temperature to 75°F (190°C) and bake for 70 minutes. When the loaf is baked, remove it from the pan and let cool on a wire rack for at least 15 to 20 minutes before slicing.

No-Knead White French Bread

This is a simple conventional bread and a good way to get familiar with the no-knead process. MAKES ONE 1½-POUND (680 G) LOAF

1 cup (240 ml) active culture from
   the Culture Proof (page 31)
1 egg, beaten
½ cup (120 ml) milk
2 tablespoons (30 g) melted butter
3½ cups (490 g) unbleached
   all-purpose flour

1 teaspoon salt
2 teaspoons sugar

GLAZE
¼ cup (60 ml) milk
Poppy seed

DOUGH PROOF In a large mixing bowl, combine the culture, egg, milk, and butter. In a separate bowl, mix together the flour, salt, and sugar. Add the dry ingredients to the liquid ingredients and mix just until a dry, firm, shaggy dough comes together, adding up to ½ cup (120 ml) more water as needed.

Cover the bowl with plastic wrap and proof for 8 to 12 hours at about 70°F (21°C). (Above 75°F/24°C, the lactobacilli are more active and the dough may become too acidic, inhibiting the wild yeast so it does not leaven as well.) After the 8- to 12-hour fermentation, the dough becomes quite sticky. With a plastic spatula, ease it away from the sides of the bowl onto a lightly floured board. Sprinkle the surface of the dough with additional flour and let it rest for 15 to 30 minutes to relax the gluten. The dough will be a very thick sticky mass; if it flattens significantly while it's resting, knead in a bit more all-purpose flour before proceeding.

LOAF PROOF With minimal handling and some additional flour (not more than ¼ cup/30 g), form a loaf and place it in a baking pan. Alternatively, form a French loaf and proof it on a baking sheet. Cover the dough with plastic wrap and proof at room temperature (70°F/21°C) for 3 to 4 hours, until doubled in bulk.

BAKING Just before baking, brush the loaf with the milk and sprinkle with poppy seed. Place the loaf in a cool oven, then turn the temperature to 375°F (190°C) and bake for 70 minutes. To increase the oven's humidity and help the loaf form a firm, chewy crust, place a pan of boiling water in the oven 10 minutes after it is turned on and spritz the oven with water several times after the first 10 minutes. When the loaf is baked, remove it from the pan and let cool on a wire rack for at least 15 to 20 minutes before slicing.

No-Knead Barm Brack

This is a popular bread in southern Ireland, and is perfect for sourdough. MAKES ONE
1¹/₂-POUND (680 G) LOAF

1 cup (240 ml) culture from the
    Culture Proof (page 31)
¹/₂ cup (120 g) melted butter
1 cup (240 ml) milk
2 eggs, beaten
3¹/₂ cups (490 g) unbleached
    all-purpose flour

1¹/₂ teaspoons salt
¹/₂ cup (120 g) brown sugar
¹/₂ teaspoon ground nutmeg
1 tablespoon caraway seed

DOUGH PROOF In a large mixing bowl, combine the culture, butter, milk, and eggs.
In a separate bowl, mix together the flour, salt, sugar, nutmeg, and caraway seed. Add
the dry ingredients to the liquid ingredients and mix just until a dry, firm, shaggy
dough comes together, adding up to ¹/₂ cup (120 ml) more water as needed.

Cover the bowl with plastic wrap and proof for 8 to 12 hours at about 70°F (21°C).
(Above 75°F/24°C, the lactobacilli are more active and the dough may become too
acidic, inhibiting the wild yeast so it does not leaven as well.) After the 8- to 12-hour
fermentation, the dough becomes quite sticky. With a plastic spatula, ease it away
from the sides of the bowl onto a lightly floured board. Sprinkle the surface of the
dough with additional flour and let it rest for 15 to 30 minutes to relax the gluten.
The dough will be a very thick sticky mass; if it flattens significantly while it's resting, knead in a bit more all-purpose flour before proceeding.

LOAF PROOF With minimal handling and some additional flour (not more than
¹/₄ cup/30 g), form a loaf and place it in a baking pan. Alternatively, form a French
loaf and proof it on a baking sheet. Cover the dough with plastic wrap and proof at
room temperature (70°F/21°C) for 3 to 4 hours, until doubled in bulk.

BAKING Place the loaf in a cool oven, then turn the temperature to 375°F (190°C)
and bake for 70 minutes. To increase the oven's humidity and help the loaf form
a firm, chewy crust, place a pan of boiling water in the oven 10 minutes after it is
turned on and spritz the oven with water several times after the first 10 minutes.
When the loaf is baked, remove it from the pan and let cool on a wire rack for at least
15 to 20 minutes before slicing.

Tanya's No-Knead Russian Black Bread

Tanya Bevan is the Russian tour guide who brought us two Russian cultures more than twenty years ago. This is an adaptation of one of her Russian recipes. As we put this recipe together, we knew it would be a very heavy loaf and probably an insurmountable challenge to the no-knead process. But the end result was mind-bogglingly good. MAKES ONE 1¹/₂-POUND (680 G) LOAF

1 cup (240 ml) culture from the Culture Proof (page 31)	¹/₂ teaspoon ground coriander
1 cup (240 ml) milk	1 tablespoon sugar
1 tablespoon dark molasses	1 cup (140 g) whole wheat flour
1 tablespoon vegetable oil	1 cup (115 g) rye flour
1 teaspoon salt	1¹/₂ cups (210 g) unbleached all-purpose flour

DOUGH PROOF In a large mixing bowl, combine the culture, milk, molasses, and vegetable oil and mix well. In a separate bowl, combine the salt, coriander, sugar, and flours and mix well. Add the dry ingredients to the liquid ingredients and mix just until a very dry, firm, shaggy dough comes together, adding up to ¹/₂ cup (120 ml) more water as needed.

Cover the bowl with plastic wrap and proof for 8 to 12 hours at about 70°F (21°C). (Above 75°F/24°C, the lactobacilli are more active and the dough may become too acidic, inhibiting the wild yeast so it does not leaven as well.) After the 8- to 12-hour fermentation, the dough becomes quite sticky. With a plastic spatula, ease it away from the sides of the bowl onto a lightly floured board. Sprinkle the surface of the dough with additional flour and let it rest for 15 to 30 minutes to relax the gluten. The dough will be a very thick sticky mass; if it flattens significantly while it's resting, knead in a bit more all-purpose flour before proceeding.

LOAF PROOF With minimal handling and some additional flour (not more than ¹/₄ cup/30 g), form a loaf and place it in a baking pan. Alternatively, form a French loaf and proof it on a baking sheet. Cover the dough with plastic wrap and proof at room temperature (70°F/21°C) for 3 to 4 hours, until doubled in bulk.

BAKING Place the loaf in a cool oven, then turn the temperature to 375°F (190°C) and bake for 70 minutes. When the loaf is baked, remove it from the pan and let cool on a wire rack for at least 15 to 20 minutes before slicing.

No-Knead German Spelt Bread

Spelt is far better known in Europe than in the United States; in Germany, it is called "din-kel." Paired with a sourdough culture, it makes a supple dough and a marvelous, flavorful loaf. In this recipe, it is combined with rye for a real taste adventure. MAKES ONE 1½-POUND (680 G) LOAF

1 cup (240 ml) culture from the
   Culture Proof (page 31)
1 tablespoon (15 g) melted butter
1 cup (240 ml) malt beer
1 teaspoon salt

1 tablespoon brown sugar
1 cup (115 g) rye flour
1 cup (130 g) white spelt flour
1½ cups (190 g) whole spelt flour

DOUGH PROOF In a large mixing bowl, combine the culture, butter, and beer and mix well. In a separate bowl, combine the salt, sugar, and flours and mix well. Add the dry ingredients to the liquid ingredients and mix just until a very dry, firm, shaggy dough comes together, adding up to ½ cup (120 ml) more water as needed.

Cover the bowl with plastic wrap and proof for 8 to 12 hours at about 70°F (21°C). (Above 75°F/24°C, the lactobacilli are more active and the dough may become too acidic, inhibiting the wild yeast so it does not leaven as well.) After the 8- to 12-hour fermentation, the dough becomes quite sticky. With a plastic spatula, ease it away from the sides of the bowl onto a lightly floured board. Sprinkle the surface of the dough with additional flour and let it rest for 15 to 30 minutes to relax the gluten. The dough will be a very thick sticky mass; if it flattens significantly while it's resting, knead in a bit more white spelt flour before proceeding.

LOAF PROOF With minimal handling and some additional flour (not more than ¼ cup/30 g), form a loaf and place it in a baking pan. Alternatively, form a French loaf and proof it on a baking sheet. Cover the dough with plastic wrap and proof at room temperature (70°F/21°C) for 3 to 4 hours, until doubled in bulk.

BAKING Place the loaf in a cool oven, then turn the temperature to 375°F (190°C) and bake for 70 minutes. To increase the oven's humidity and help the loaf form a firm, chewy crust, place a pan of boiling water in the oven 10 minutes after it is turned on and spritz the oven with water several times after the first 10 minutes. When the loaf is baked, remove it from the pan and let cool on a wire rack for at least 15 to 20 minutes before slicing.

No-Knead Kamut Bread

Kamut may not have originated in ancient Egypt as its modern proponents originally thought, but it is a venerable wheat. Agronomists are inclined to classify it as a subtype of durum. Regardless of its origins, it imparts a distinctly nutty flavor to a sourdough loaf.

MAKES ONE 1½-POUND (680 G) LOAF

1 cup (240 ml) culture from the
    Culture Proof (page 31)
2 tablespoons oil
1 cup (240 ml) water
1 teaspoon salt
1 tablespoon sugar

1 tablespoon caraway seed
1 cup (115 g) rye flour
1 cup (130 g) Kamut flour
2 cups (280 g) unbleached
    all-purpose flour

DOUGH PROOF In a large mixing bowl, combine the culture, oil, and water and mix well. In a separate bowl, combine the salt, sugar, caraway seed, and flours and mix well. Add the dry ingredients to the liquid ingredients and mix just until a very dry, firm, shaggy dough comes together, adding up to ½ cup (120 ml) more water as needed.

Cover the bowl with plastic wrap and proof for 8 to 12 hours at about 70°F (21°C). (Above 75°F/24°C, the lactobacilli are more active and the dough may become too acidic, inhibiting the wild yeast so it does not leaven as well.) After the 8- to 12-hour fermentation, the dough becomes quite sticky. With a plastic spatula, ease it away from the sides of the bowl onto a lightly floured board. Sprinkle the surface of the dough with additional flour and let it rest for 15 to 30 minutes to relax the gluten. The dough will be a very thick sticky mass; if it flattens significantly while it's resting, knead in a bit more all-purpose flour before proceeding.

LOAF PROOF With minimal handling and some additional flour (not more than ¼ cup/30 g), form a loaf and place it in a baking pan. Alternatively, form a French loaf and proof it on a baking sheet. Cover the dough with plastic wrap and proof at room temperature (70°F/21°C) for 3 to 4 hours, until doubled in bulk.

BAKING Place the loaf in a cool oven, then turn the temperature to 375°F (190°C) and bake for 70 minutes. To increase the oven's humidity and help the loaf form a firm, chewy crust, place a pan of boiling water in the oven 10 minutes after it is turned on and spritz the oven with water several times after the first 10 minutes. When the loaf is baked, remove it from the pan and let cool on a wire rack for at least 15 to 20 minutes before slicing.

Kamut Bread

Kamut is related to durum; this perhaps is an explanation for its relatively poor gluten content. One cup (130 g) of it can substitute in any recipe for 1 cup of rye flour (115 g) or whole wheat flour (140 g). MAKES ONE 1¹/₂-POUND (680 G) LOAF

1 cup (240 ml) culture from the
   Culture Proof (page 31)
1 teaspoon salt
1 tablespoon sugar
2 tablespoons oil
1 tablespoon caraway seed

1 cup (240 ml) warm water
³/₄ cup (85 g) rye flour
³/₄ cup (100 g) Kamut flour
2 cups (280 g) unbleached
   all-purpose flour

DOUGH PROOF Pour the culture into a mixing bowl. In a separate bowl, stir the salt, sugar, oil, and caraway seed into the warm water and then add to the culture. Add the rye and Kamut flours and mix well. Add the all-purpose flour a cup (140 g) at a time until the dough is too stiff to mix by hand. Turn out onto a floured board and knead in the remaining flour until the dough is smooth and satiny.

Or mix and knead all of the ingredients for a maximum of 25 minutes in a bread machine or other mixer (see page 152).

Proof the dough overnight (8 to 12 hours) at room temperature, about 70°F (21°C), in a large bowl covered with plastic wrap (or leave in the machine pan, removed from the machine, securing the plastic wrap with a rubber band). During this time, the dough should double in size in the covered bowl, or rise to the top of the machine pan. After the proof, use a spatula to gently ease the dough out onto a floured board. Allow the dough to rest for 30 minutes. If marked flattening occurs during this time, knead in additional flour before shaping.

LOAF PROOF To shape the rested dough, flatten it slightly, then lift a portion from the periphery and pull it toward the center. Continue this around the dough mass to form a rough ball (see page 34), then pat and pull into the loaf shape you desire. Place the shaped loaf in a bread pan or on a baking sheet and proof for 2 to 4 hours, until it reaches nearly to the top of the pan or doubles in bulk. Proof for the first hour at room temperature and then at 85° to 90°F (29° to 32°C) in a proofing box.

BAKING Place the pan with its shaped, proofed loaf in a cool oven, then turn the temperature to 375°F (190°C) and bake for 70 minutes. When the loaf is baked, remove it from the pan and let cool on a wire rack for at least 15 to 20 minutes before slicing.

Prairie Flax Bread

This recipe comes out of Manitoba flax country. When you want to increase your intake of omega-3 fatty acids and can't afford to eat salmon four times a week, this bread will serve you well. **MAKES TWO 1½-POUND (680 G) LOAVES**

2 cups (480 ml) culture from the
   Culture Proof (page 31)
1¼ cups (300 ml) water
1½ teaspoons salt
3 tablespoons (45 ml) honey
3 tablespoons (45 ml) vegetable oil

2 tablespoons sunflower seeds
¼ cup (35 g) flaxseed
1 tablespoon poppy seed
½ cup (60 g) flax flour
4¼ cups (595 g) unbleached
   all-purpose flour

DOUGH PROOF Pour the culture into a mixing bowl. Add the water, salt, honey, and oil and mix. In a separate small bowl, combine the sunflower seeds, flaxseed, and poppy seed, then add to the culture mixture. Mix in the flax flour, then add the all-purpose flour a cup (140 g) at a time until the dough is too stiff to mix by hand. Turn out onto a floured board and knead in the remaining flour until the dough is smooth and satiny.

Proof the dough overnight (8 to 12 hours) at room temperature, about 70°F (21°C), in a large bowl covered with plastic wrap. During this time, the dough should double in size. After the proof, use a spatula to gently ease the dough out onto a floured board. Allow the dough to rest for 30 minutes. If marked flattening occurs during this time, knead in additional flour before shaping.

LOAF PROOF To shape the rested dough, divide it in half, then shape it into 2 balls, and pat and pull into the loaf shape you desire. Place the shaped loaves on a baking sheet or in pans and proof for 2 to 4 hours, until they double in bulk or nearly reach the tops of the pans. Proof for the first hour at room temperature and then at 85° to 90°F (29° to 32°C) in a proofing box.

BAKING Place the pans with their shaped, proofed loaves in a cool oven, then turn the temperature to 375°F (190°C) and bake for 70 minutes. When the loaves are baked, remove them from the pans and let cool on a wire rack for at least 15 to 20 minutes before slicing.

Basic Durum Bread

You can use durum as a complete substitute for whole wheat flours in any recipe in this book. As with any whole wheat, better leavening will occur with about 50 percent white bread flour, but we have successfully used durum with only 25 percent white flour. The flavor of durum is hard to resist. This is the recipe to sample the unique taste of durum without the masking flavors of other ingredients. MAKES ONE 1½-POUND (680 G) LOAF

1 cup (240 ml) culture from the
    Culture Proof (page 31)
1 tablespoon (15 g) butter
1 cup (240 ml) milk
³/₄ teaspoon salt

1 tablespoon sugar
1½ cups (210 g) durum flour
1½ cups (210 g) unbleached
    all-purpose flour

DOUGH PROOF Pour the culture into a mixing bowl. Melt the butter and add the milk to warm. Stir in the salt and sugar until dissolved. Add this mixture to the culture and mix well. Mix in the durum flour. Add the all-purpose flour a cup (140 g) at a time until the dough is too stiff to mix by hand. Turn out onto a floured board and knead in the remaining flour until the dough is smooth and satiny.

Or mix and knead all of the ingredients for a maximum of 25 minutes in a bread machine or other mixer (see page 152).

Proof the dough overnight (8 to 12 hours) at room temperature, about 70°F (21°C), in a large bowl covered with plastic wrap (or leave in the machine pan, removed from the machine, securing the plastic wrap with a rubber band). During this time, the dough should double in size in the covered bowl, or rise to the top of the machine pan. After the proof, use a spatula to gently ease the dough out onto a floured board. Allow the dough to rest for 30 minutes. If marked flattening occurs during this time, knead in additional flour before shaping.

LOAF PROOF To shape the rested dough, flatten it slightly, then lift a portion from the periphery and pull it toward the center. Continue this around the dough mass to form a rough ball (see page 34), then pat and pull the ball into an oval 1 inch (2.5 cm) thick. Form a loaf by rolling from the long side, pinching the seam together as you roll the dough to form the loaf. Place the loaf, seam side down, in a bread pan. Proof for the first hour at room temperature and then at 85° to 90°F (29° to 32°C) in a proofing box.

BAKING Place the pan with its shaped, proofed loaf in a cool oven, then turn the temperature to 375°F (190°C) and bake for 70 minutes. When the loaf is baked, remove it from the pan and let cool on a wire rack for at least 15 to 20 minutes before slicing.

Durum Rye Bread

We've raved about the taste of durum in bread, but you'll think we've understated it when you taste this bread. MAKES ONE 1½-POUND (680 G) LOAF

1 cup (240 ml) culture from the
   Culture Proof (page 31)
1 cup (240 ml) milk
1 teaspoon salt
2 tablespoons brown sugar

1 tablespoon (15 g) melted butter or oil
¾ cup (85 g) rye flour
1¼ cups (175 g) durum flour
1½ cups (210 g) unbleached
   all-purpose flour

DOUGH PROOF Pour the culture into a mixing bowl. Add the milk, salt, sugar, and butter and mix well. Add the rye and durum flours and mix. Add the all-purpose flour a cup (140 g) at a time until the dough is too stiff to mix by hand. Turn out onto a floured board and knead in the remaining flour until the dough is smooth and satiny.

Or mix and knead all of the ingredients for a maximum of 25 minutes in a bread machine or other mixer (see page 152).

Proof the dough overnight (8 to 12 hours) at room temperature, about 70°F (21°C), in a large bowl covered with plastic wrap (or leave in the machine pan, removed from the machine, securing the plastic wrap with a rubber band). During this time, the dough should double in size in the covered bowl, or rise to the top of the machine pan. After the proof, use a spatula to gently ease the dough out onto a floured board. Allow the dough to rest for 30 minutes. If marked flattening occurs during this time, knead in additional flour before shaping.

LOAF PROOF To shape the rested dough, flatten it slightly, then lift a portion from the periphery and pull it toward the center. Continue this around the dough mass to form a rough ball (see page 34), then pat and pull into the loaf shape you desire. Place the shaped loaf in a bread pan or on a baking sheet and proof for 2 to 4 hours, until it reaches nearly to the top of the pan or doubles in bulk. Proof for the first hour at room temperature and then at 85° to 90°F (29° to 32°C) in a proofing box.

BAKING Just before baking, make crisscross slashes in the dough with a razor blade. Place the pan with its shaped, proofed loaf in a cool oven, then turn the temperature to 375°F (190°C) and bake for 65 to 70 minutes. When the loaf is baked, remove it from the pan and let cool on a wire rack for at least 15 to 20 minutes before slicing.

Durum Sunflower Bread

To add the health advantages of soy to this loaf, you can substitute soy flour for the durum flour. MAKES ONE 1¹/₂-POUND (680 G) LOAF

1 cup (240 ml) culture from the
  Culture Proof (page 31)
1 tablespoon (15 g) butter
1 cup (240 ml) milk
1 teaspoon salt
1 tablespoon honey

¹/₂ cup (50 g) raw sunflower seeds
1 cup (140 g) durum flour
1¹/₄ cups (175 g) whole wheat flour
1¹/₄ cups (175 g) unbleached
  all-purpose flour

DOUGH PROOF Pour the culture into a mixing bowl. Melt the butter and add the milk to warm it. Stir in the salt, honey, and sunflower seeds, then add this mixture to the culture and mix well. Add the durum and whole wheat flours. Add the all-purpose flour a cup (140 g) at a time until the dough is too stiff to mix by hand. Turn out onto a floured board and knead in the remaining flour until smooth and satiny.

Or mix and knead all of the ingredients for a maximum of 25 minutes in a bread machine or other mixer (see page 152).

Proof the dough overnight (8 to 12 hours) at room temperature, about 70°F (21°C), in a large bowl covered with plastic wrap (or leave in the machine pan, removed from the machine, securing the plastic wrap with a rubber band). During this time, the dough should double in size in the covered bowl, or rise to the top of the machine pan. After the proof, use a spatula to gently ease the dough out onto a floured board. Allow the dough to rest for 30 minutes. If marked flattening occurs during this time, knead in additional flour before shaping.

LOAF PROOF To shape the rested dough, flatten it slightly, then lift a portion from the periphery and pull it toward the center. Continue this around the dough mass to form a rough ball (see page 34), then pat and pull into the loaf shape you desire. Place the shaped dough in a bread pan or on a baking sheet and proof for 2 to 4 hours, until it reaches nearly to the top of the pan or doubles in bulk. Proof for the first hour at room temperature and then at 85° to 90°F (29° to 32°C) in a proofing box.

BAKING Place the pan with its shaped, proofed loaf in a cool oven, then turn the temperature to 375°F (190°C) and bake for 65 to 70 minutes. When the loaf is baked, remove it from the pan and let cool on a wire rack for at least 15 to 20 minutes before slicing.

Spelt Bread

This and the spelt recipes that follow all use various combinations of white and whole spelt flours. Some also include rye and whole wheat flours; you can also use spelt as a substitute in rye and whole wheat breads, or as an addition. You should note the caution that spelt flours have a "short mixing tolerance," but I have not experienced a problem with this in my use of spelt. If your breads do not rise well, however, you may need to experiment with kneading less. This is a good recipe to compare the qualities of spelt and Kamut, another ancient grain that makes an excellent addition to many sourdough breads. MAKES ONE 1½-POUND (680 G) LOAF

1 cup (240 ml) culture from the Culture Proof (page 31)	1 cup (240 ml) warm water
1 teaspoon salt	³/₄ cup (85 g) rye flour
1 tablespoon sugar	³/₄ cup (100 g) white spelt flour
2 tablespoons oil	2 cups (280 g) unbleached all-purpose flour
1 tablespoon caraway seed	

DOUGH PROOF Pour the culture into a mixing bowl. Add the salt, sugar, oil, and caraway seed to the water, mix briefly, and add to the culture. Add the rye and spelt flours and mix well. Add the all-purpose flour until the dough is too stiff to mix by hand. Turn out onto a floured board and knead in the remaining flour until the dough is smooth and satiny.

Or mix and knead all of the ingredients for a maximum of 25 minutes in a bread machine or other mixer (see page 152).

Proof the dough overnight (8 to 12 hours) at room temperature, about 70°F (21°C), in a large bowl covered with plastic wrap (or leave in the machine pan, removed from the machine, securing the plastic wrap with a rubber band). During this time, the dough should double in size in the covered bowl, or rise to the top of the machine pan. After the proof, use a spatula to gently ease the dough out onto a floured board. Allow the dough to rest for 30 minutes. If marked flattening occurs during this time, knead in additional flour before shaping.

LOAF PROOF To shape the rested dough, flatten it slightly, then lift a portion from the periphery and pull it toward the center. Continue this around the dough mass to form a rough ball (see page 34), then pat and pull into the loaf shape you desire. Place the shaped loaf on a baking sheet or in a pan and proof for 2 to 4 hours, until it doubles in bulk or reaches nearly the top of the pan. Proof for the first hour at room temperature and then at 85° to 90°F (29° to 32°C) in a proofing box.

BAKING Place the pan with its shaped, proofed loaf in a cool oven, then turn the temperature to 375°F (190°C) and bake for 70 minutes. When the loaf is baked, remove it from the pan and let cool on a wire rack for at least 15 to 20 minutes before slicing.

German Spelt Bread

In this bread, whole and white spelt flours substitute wholly for regular wheat flour, and rye and beer yield a loaf with classic European flavors. MAKES ONE 1½-POUND (680 G) LOAF

1 cup (240 ml) culture from the
   Culture Proof (page 31)
1 tablespoon (15 g) butter
1 cup (240 ml) malt beer
1 teaspoon salt

1 tablespoon brown sugar
1 cup (115 g) rye flour
1½ cups (190 g) whole spelt flour
1 cup (130 g) white spelt flour

DOUGH PROOF Pour the culture into a mixing bowl. Melt the butter and stir in the beer, salt, and brown sugar. Add this mixture to the culture and stir well. Mix in the rye flour and the whole spelt flour. Add the white spelt flour and mix, turning it out onto a floured board to knead in the flour as necessary; keep kneading until the dough is smooth and satiny.

Or mix and knead all of the ingredients for a maximum of 25 minutes in a bread machine or other mixer (see page 152).

Proof the dough overnight (8 to 12 hours) at room temperature, about 70°F (21°C), in a large bowl covered with plastic wrap (or leave in the machine pan, removed from the machine, securing the plastic wrap with a rubber band). During this time, the dough should double in size in the covered bowl, or rise to the top of the machine pan. After the proof, use a spatula to gently ease the dough out onto a floured board. Allow the dough to rest for 30 minutes. If marked flattening occurs during this time, knead in additional flour before shaping.

LOAF PROOF To shape the rested dough, flatten it slightly, then lift a portion from the periphery and pull it toward the center. Continue this around the dough mass to form a rough ball (see page 34), then pat and pull into the loaf shape you desire. Place the shaped loaf on a baking sheet or in a pan and proof for 2 to 4 hours, until it doubles in bulk or rises nearly to the top of the pan. Proof for the first hour at room temperature and then at 85° to 90°F (29° to 32°C) in a proofing box.

BAKING Place the pan with its shaped, proofed loaf in a cool oven, then turn the temperature to 375°F (190°C) and bake for 70 minutes. When the loaf is baked, remove it from the pan and let cool on a wire rack for at least 15 to 20 minutes before slicing.

Austrian Spelt Bread

Molasses and brown sugar give this bread an exceptional flavor. MAKES ONE 1½-POUND (680 G) LOAF

1 cup (240 ml) culture from the Culture Proof (page 31)	1 tablespoon oil
1 teaspoon salt	1½ teaspoons caraway seed
1 tablespoon brown sugar	1 tablespoon fennel seed
1 cup (240 ml) water	¾ cup (85 g) medium rye flour
1 tablespoon molasses	¾ cup (105 g) whole wheat flour
	2 cups (255 g) white spelt flour

DOUGH PROOF Pour the culture into a mixing bowl. Dissolve the salt and sugar in the water, then add the molasses, oil, caraway seed, and fennel seed and mix well. Stir this mixture into the culture. Combine the rye and whole wheat flours and mix into the culture. Add a cup (130 g) of the spelt flour and mix. Turn out onto a floured board and knead in the remaining spelt flour until the dough is smooth and shiny.

Or mix and knead all of the ingredients for a maximum of 25 minutes in a bread machine or other mixer (see page 152).

Proof the dough overnight (8 to 12 hours) at room temperature, about 70°F (21°C), in a large bowl covered with plastic wrap (or leave in the machine pan, removed from the machine, securing the plastic wrap with a rubber band). During this time, the dough should double in size in the covered bowl, or rise to the top of the machine pan. After the proof, use a spatula to gently ease the dough out onto a floured board. Allow the dough to rest for 30 minutes. If marked flattening occurs during this time, knead in additional flour before shaping.

LOAF PROOF To shape the rested dough, flatten it slightly, then lift a portion from the periphery and pull it toward the center. Continue this around the dough mass to form a rough ball (see page 34), then pat and pull into a pan loaf or French loaf. Place the shaped loaf on a baking sheet or in a pan and proof for 2 to 4 hours, until it doubles in bulk or rises nearly to the top of the pan. Proof for the first hour at room temperature and then at 85° to 90°F (29° to 32°C) in a proofing box.

BAKING Place the pan with its shaped, proofed loaf in a cool oven, then turn the temperature to 375°F (190°C) and bake for 70 minutes. When the loaf is baked, remove it from the pan and let cool on a wire rack for at least 15 to 20 minutes before slicing.

Caraway Spelt Bread

Spelt produces a rich, creamy texture when added to a sourdough culture, and the physical difference between spelt flour and wheat flours is immediately obvious. The flavor of caraway with spelt is equally unique. MAKES ONE 1½-POUND (680 G) LOAF

1 cup (240 ml) culture from the
  Culture Proof (page 31)
1 cup (240 ml) water
1 tablespoon (15 g) melted butter
1 tablespoon molasses

1 teaspoon salt
1 tablespoon caraway seed
1 cup (115 g) rye flour
2½ cups (320 g) white spelt flour

DOUGH PROOF Pour the culture into a mixing bowl. Mix in the water, butter, molasses, salt, and caraway seed. Add the rye flour and mix. Add the spelt flour a cup (130 g) at a time until the dough is too stiff to mix by hand. Turn out onto a floured board and knead in the remaining flour until the dough is smooth and satiny.

Or mix and knead all of the ingredients for a maximum of 25 minutes in a bread machine or other mixer (see page 152).

Proof the dough overnight (8 to 12 hours) at room temperature, about 70°F (21°C), in a large bowl covered with plastic wrap (or leave in the machine pan, removed from the machine, securing the plastic wrap with a rubber band). During this time, the dough should double in size in the covered bowl, or rise to the top of the machine pan. After the proof, use a spatula to gently ease the dough out onto a floured board. Allow the dough to rest for 30 minutes. If marked flattening occurs during this time, knead in additional flour before shaping.

LOAF PROOF To shape the rested dough, flatten it slightly, then lift a portion from the periphery and pull it toward the center. Continue this around the dough mass to form a rough ball (see page 34), then pat and pull into the loaf shape you desire. Place the shaped loaf on a baking sheet or in a pan and proof for 2 to 4 hours, until it doubles in bulk or rises to the top of the pan. Proof for the first hour at room temperature and then at 85° to 90°F (29° to 32°C) in a proofing box.

BAKING Place the pan with its shaped, proofed loaf in a cool oven, then turn the temperature to 375°F (190°C) and bake for 70 minutes. When the loaf is baked, remove it from the pan and let cool on a wire rack for at least 15 to 20 minutes before slicing.

Herb Spelt Bread

This recipe, which uses only white spelt flour, enables you to compare the leavening char-acteristics and flavor of spelt with those of wheat flours. MAKES ONE 1½-POUND (680 G) LOAF

1 cup (240 ml) culture from the
   Culture Proof (page 31)
1 tablespoon (15 g) butter or oil
1 cup (240 ml) milk
1 teaspoon salt

1 tablespoon sugar
1 teaspoon dried thyme
1 teaspoon dried oregano
1 teaspoon crushed dried basil
3½ cups (450 g) white spelt flour

DOUGH PROOF Pour the culture into a mixing bowl. Melt the butter (or warm the oil) over moderate heat and add the milk to warm. Stir in the salt, sugar, and herbs and add this mixture to the culture; mix well. Add the flour 1 cup (130 g) at a time until the dough is too stiff to mix by hand. Turn out onto a floured board and knead in the remaining flour until the dough is smooth and satiny.

Or mix and knead all of the ingredients for a maximum of 25 minutes in a bread machine or other mixer (see page 152).

Proof the dough overnight (8 to 12 hours) at room temperature, about 70°F (21°C), in a large bowl covered with plastic wrap (or leave in the machine pan, removed from the machine, securing the plastic wrap with a rubber band). During this time, the dough should double in size in the covered bowl, or rise to the top of the machine pan. After the proof, use a spatula to gently ease the dough out onto a floured board. Allow the dough to rest for 30 minutes. If marked flattening occurs during this time, knead in additional flour before shaping.

LOAF PROOF To shape the rested dough, flatten it slightly, then lift a portion from the periphery and pull it toward the center. Continue this around the dough mass to form a rough ball (see page 34), then pat and pull into the loaf shape you desire. Place the shaped loaf on a baking sheet or in a pan and proof for 2 to 4 hours, until it doubles in bulk or rises almost to the top of the pan. Proof for the first hour at room temperature and then at 85° to 90°F (29° to 32°C) in a proofing box.

BAKING Place the pan with its shaped, proofed loaf in a cool oven, then turn the temperature to 375°F (190°C) and bake for 70 minutes. When the loaf is baked, remove it from the pan and let cool on a wire rack for at least 15 to 20 minutes before slicing.

Cinnamon Spelt Rolls

Brush the tops of these rolls with either melted butter or a glaze of confectioners' sugar, milk, and vanilla. MAKES 12 TO 14 ROLLS

1 cup (240 ml) culture from the
   Culture Proof (page 31)
1 cup (240 ml) milk
$^1/_2$ teaspoon vanilla extract
1 teaspoon salt
1 tablespoon plus 2 teaspoons sugar
3$^1/_2$ cups (450 g) white spelt flour
1 tablespoon (15 g) melted butter
2 teaspoons ground cinnamon
$^1/_2$ cup (80 g) raisins

GLAZES
2 tablespoons (30 g) melted butter
   (optional)

1 cup (140 g) confectioners' sugar
   (optional)
4 teaspoons hot milk (optional)
$^1/_2$ teaspoon vanilla extract
   (optional)

DOUGH PROOF Pour the culture into a mixing bowl. Add the milk, vanilla, salt, and 1 tablespoon of the sugar to the culture and mix well. Add the flour a cup (130 g) at a time until the dough has become too stiff to mix by hand. Turn out onto floured board and knead in the remaining flour until the dough is smooth and satiny.

Or mix and knead the ingredients for a maximum of 25 minutes in a bread machine or other mixer (see page 152).

Proof the dough overnight (8 to 12 hours) at room temperature, about 70°F (21°C), in a large bowl covered with plastic wrap (or leave in the machine pan, removed from the machine, securing the plastic wrap with a rubber band). During this time, the dough should double in size in the covered bowl, or rise to the top of the machine pan. After the proof, use a spatula to gently ease the dough out onto a floured board. Allow the dough to rest for 30 minutes. If marked flattening occurs during this time, knead in additional flour before shaping.

LOAF PROOF Roll the rested dough into a rectangle about $^1/_2$ inch (1.5 cm) thick. Brush the surface with the melted butter. Mix the remaining 2 teaspoons sugar with the cinnamon and sprinkle this mixture over the loaf. Spread the raisins evenly over the loaf. Roll up the rectangle from the long side and cut the roll into rolls 1 inch (2.5 cm) thick. Place the rolls close together on a baking sheet and proof at 85°F (29°C) in a proofing box for 2 to 4 hours, until the rolls double in bulk.

BAKING Bake the rolls in a preheated oven at 400°F (200°C) for 25 to 30 minutes. Remove the rolls to a wire rack to cool; while they are hot, either brush the tops with the 2 tablespoons melted butter or drizzle with a glaze made of the confectioners' sugar, hot milk, and vanilla. If the glaze is too stiff for drizzling, add milk, a few drops at a time, to thin it.

Finnish Rye Bread

Brown sugar imparts a golden brown color and enhances the flavor of this moderately heavy rye bread, which may rise slowly. It is a favorite in Scandinavia, where long winter nights give plenty of time for proofing. MAKES ONE 1½-POUND (680 G) LOAF

1 cup (240 ml) culture from the
 Culture Proof (page 31)
1 cup (240 ml) milk
1½ teaspoons salt
¼ cup (60 g) dark brown sugar

2 tablespoons (30 g) melted butter
1½ cups (170 g) rye flour
2 cups (280 g) unbleached
 all-purpose flour

DOUGH PROOF Pour the culture into a mixing bowl. Add the milk, salt, sugar, and butter and mix. Add the rye flour and mix. Add the all-purpose flour a cup (140 g) at a time until the dough is too stiff to mix by hand. Turn out onto a floured board and knead in the remaining flour until the dough is smooth and satiny.

Or mix and knead all of the ingredients for a maximum of 25 minutes in a bread machine or other mixer (see page 152).

Proof the dough overnight (8 to 12 hours) at room temperature, about 70°F (21°C), in a large bowl covered with plastic wrap (or leave in the machine pan, removed from the machine, securing the plastic wrap with a rubber band). During this time, the dough should double in size in the covered bowl, or rise to the top of the machine pan. After the proof, use a spatula to gently ease the dough out onto a floured board. Allow the dough to rest for 30 minutes. If marked flattening occurs during this time, knead in additional flour before shaping.

LOAF PROOF To shape the rested dough, flatten it slightly, then lift a portion from the periphery and pull it toward the center. Continue this around the dough mass to form a rough ball (see page 34), then pat and pull into the loaf shape you desire. Place the shaped loaf on a baking sheet or in a bread pan and proof for 2 to 4 hours, until it doubles in bulk or reaches nearly to the top of the pan. Proof for the first hour at room temperature and at 85° to 90°F (29° to 32°C) in a proofing box.

BAKING Just before baking, make crisscross slashes in the top of the loaf with a razor blade. Place the pan with its shaped, proofed loaf in a cool oven, then turn the temperature to 375°F (190°C) and bake for 70 minutes. When the loaf is baked, remove it from the pan and let cool on a wire rack for at least 15 to 20 minutes before slicing.

Raisin Rye Bread

This is an excellent bread for breakfast toast. For variety, substitute whole wheat flour for the rye flour and use two tablespoons of brown sugar instead of the white sugar. MAKES ONE 1¹/₂-POUND (680 G) LOAF

1 cup (240 ml) culture from the
  Culture Proof (page 31)
1 cup (240 ml) water
1 teaspoon salt
1 tablespoon sugar
1 tablespoon oil
1 cup (150 g) raisins, soaked 30 minutes
  in warm water and drained

1¹/₂ cups (170 g) rye flour
2 cups (280 g) unbleached
  all-purpose flour
1 egg, beaten
1 tablespoon milk

DOUGH PROOF Pour the culture into a mixing bowl. Add the water, salt, sugar, oil, and raisins and mix well. Add the rye flour and mix well. Add the all-purpose flour a cup (140 g) at a time until the dough is too stiff to mix by hand. Turn out onto a floured board and knead in the remaining flour until the dough is smooth and satiny.

Or mix and knead all of the ingredients for a maximum of 25 minutes in a bread machine or other mixer (see page 152).

Proof the dough overnight (8 to 12 hours) at room temperature, about 70°F (21°C), in a large bowl covered with plastic wrap (or leave in the machine pan, removed from the machine, securing the plastic wrap with a rubber band). During this time, the dough should double in size in the covered bowl, or rise to the top of the machine pan. After the proof, use a spatula to gently ease the dough out onto a floured board. Allow the dough to rest for 30 minutes. If marked flattening occurs during this time, knead in additional flour before shaping.

LOAF PROOF To shape the rested dough, flatten it slightly, then lift a portion from the periphery and pull it toward the center. Continue this around the dough mass to form a rough ball (see page 34), then pat and pull into the loaf shape you desire. Place the shaped loaf on a sheet or in a bread pan and proof for 2 to 4 hours, until it doubles in bulk. Proof for the first hour at room temperature and then at 85° to 90°F (29° to 32°C) in a proofing box.

continued

Raisin Rye Bread, *continued*

BAKING Just before baking, combine the beaten egg with the milk and brush the top of the loaf with this glaze. Place the pan with its shaped, proofed loaf in a cool oven, then turn the temperature to 375°F (190°C) and bake for 70 minutes. Or transfer the loaf to a preheated baking stone in a 450°F (230°C) oven and bake for 40 minutes. When the loaf is baked, remove it from the pan and let cool on a wire rack for at least 15 to 20 minutes before slicing.

Sour Cream Rye Bread

This is a heavy rye dough that will rise slowly; if it doesn't rise enough the first time you do it, consider using Vital Gluten (see page 23). With an aggressive culture, you probably won't need it. MAKES ONE 1½-POUND (680 G) LOAF

1 cup (240 ml) culture from the
    Culture Proof (page 31)
1½ teaspoons salt
2 teaspoons sugar
1 tablespoon oil

1½ cups (360 g) sour cream
1 tablespoon caraway seed
1½ cups (170 g) rye flour
2 cups (280 g) unbleached
    all-purpose flour

DOUGH PROOF Pour the culture into a mixing bowl. Add the salt, sugar, oil, sour cream, and caraway seed and mix well. Add the rye flour and mix. Add the all-purpose flour a cup (140 g) at a time until the dough is too stiff to mix by hand. Turn out onto a floured board and knead in the remaining flour until the dough is smooth and satiny.

Or mix and knead all of the ingredients for a maximum of 25 minutes in a bread machine or other mixer (see page 152).

Proof the dough overnight (8 to 12 hours) at room temperature, about 70°F (21°C), in a large bowl covered with plastic wrap (or leave in the machine pan, removed from the machine, securing the plastic wrap with a rubber band). During this time, the dough should double in size in the covered bowl, or rise to the top of the machine pan. After the proof, use a spatula to gently ease the dough out onto a floured board. Allow the dough to rest for 30 minutes. If marked flattening occurs during this time, knead in additional flour before shaping.

LOAF PROOF To shape the rested dough, flatten it slightly, then lift a portion from the periphery and pull it toward the center. Continue this around the dough mass to form a rough ball (see page 34), then pat and pull into the loaf shape you desire. Place the shaped loaf in a bread pan or on a baking sheet and proof for 2 to 5 hours, until it reaches nearly to the top of the pan or doubles in bulk. Proof for the first hour at room temperature and then at 85° to 90°F (29° to 32°C) in a proofing box.

BAKING Place the pan with its shaped, proofed loaf in a cool oven, then turn the temperature to 375°F (190°C) and bake for 70 minutes. Or transfer the loaf to a pre-heated baking stone in a 450°F (230°C) oven and bake for 40 minutes. When the loaf is baked, remove it from the pan and let cool on a wire rack for at least 15 to 20 minutes before slicing.

Caraway Rye Bread

There are few better combinations in bread baking than caraway and rye. And though many of these rye recipes utilize caraway, this one in particular enhances the combination of these two flavors. A cup (85 g) of soy flour may be substituted for one cup (115 g) of rye flour or for one cup (140 g) of white flour. MAKES TWO 1½-POUND (680 G) LOAVES

2 cups (480 ml) culture from the Culture Proof (page 31)	2 tablespoons caraway seed
1 cup (240 ml) water	2 cups (220 g) light rye flour
2 tablespoons (30 g) butter	4 cups (560 g) unbleached all-purpose flour
2 teaspoons salt	1 egg, beaten
¾ cup (180 ml) dark molasses	1 tablespoon milk

DOUGH PROOF Pour the culture into a mixing bowl. Add the water, butter, salt, molasses, and caraway seed and mix. Add the rye flour and mix. Add the all-purpose flour a cup (140 g) at a time until the dough is too stiff to mix by hand. Turn out onto a floured board and knead in the remaining flour until the dough is smooth and satiny.

Proof the dough overnight (8 to 12 hours) at room temperature, about 70°F (21°C), in a large bowl covered with plastic wrap. During this time, the dough should double in size. After the proof, use a spatula to gently ease the dough out onto a floured board. Allow the dough to rest for 30 minutes. If marked flattening occurs during this time, knead in additional flour before shaping.

LOAF PROOF Divide the rested dough in half and form it into 2 balls. Press the balls into flat ovals 1 inch (2.5 cm) thick and roll the ovals into loaves, pinching the seams as the rolls progress. Place the shaped loaves on a baking sheet or in bread pans and proof for 2 to 4 hours, until doubled in bulk or almost level with the tops of the pans. Proof for the first hour at room temperature and then at 85° to 90°F (29° to 32°C) in a proofing box.

BAKING Just before baking, combine the beaten egg and milk and brush the tops of the loaves with this glaze. Bake in a preheated oven at 400°F (200°C) for 55 minutes. Remove the loaves from the pans and let cool on wire racks for at least 15 to 20 minutes before slicing.

German Rye Bread

For those who prefer a more subtle and delicate rye flavor, a single cup (115 g) of rye flour is ideal. This bread rises well and is a favorite in southern Austria as well as in Germany.

MAKES TWO 1½-POUND (680 G) LOAVES

2 cups (480 ml) culture from the
    Culture Proof (page 31)
1 cup (240 ml) milk
2 teaspoons salt
2 tablespoons molasses
2 tablespoons oil

1 cup (115 g) rye flour
5 cups (700 g) unbleached
    all-purpose flour
1 egg, beaten
Caraway seed

DOUGH PROOF Pour the culture into a mixing bowl. Add the milk, salt, molasses, and oil and mix. Add the rye flour and mix. Add the all-purpose flour a cup (140 g) at a time until the dough is too stiff to mix by hand. Turn out onto a floured board and knead in the remaining flour until the dough is smooth and satiny.

Proof the dough overnight (8 to 12 hours) at room temperature, about 70°F (21°C), in a large bowl covered with plastic wrap. During this time, the dough should double in size. After the proof, use a spatula to gently ease the dough out onto a floured board. Allow the dough to rest for 30 minutes. If marked flattening occurs during this time, knead in additional flour before shaping.

LOAF PROOF Divide the rested dough in half and shape by flattening it slightly, then lift a portion from the periphery and pull it toward the center. Continue this around the dough mass to form a rough ball (see page 34), then pat and pull into the loaf shape you desire. Proof for 2 to 4 hours, until almost doubled in bulk or almost level with the tops of the pans. Proof for the first hour at room temperature and then at 85° to 90°F (29° to 32°C) in a proofing box.

BAKING Just before baking, brush the loaves with the beaten egg and sprinkle with caraway seed. With a razor blade, make diagonal slashes on pan loaves or crisscross slashes on oval loaves. Place the pan with its shaped, proofed loaves in a cool oven, then turn the temperature to 375°F (190°C) and bake for 70 minutes. Or transfer the loaves to a preheated baking stone in a 450°F (230°C) oven and bake for 40 minutes. When the loaves are baked, remove from the pan and let cool on a wire rack for at least 15 to 20 minutes before slicing.

Austrian Wheat Rye Bread

The combination of white and rye flours produces a moderate rye flavor. The bread rises well but will result in a somewhat heavier loaf. The anise and caraway impart the typical flavor so characteristic of European rye bread. MAKES ONE 1½-POUND (680 G) LOAF

1 cup (240 ml) culture from the
   Culture Proof (page 31)
1 cup (240 ml) milk
1½ teaspoons salt
1 tablespoon sugar
½ tablespoon caraway seed

½ teaspoon anise seed
½ teaspoon ground cumin
1 cup (115 g) rye flour
2½ cups (350 g) unbleached
   all-purpose flour

DOUGH PROOF Pour the culture into a mixing bowl. Add the milk, salt, sugar, and spices and mix. Add the rye flour and mix well. Add the all-purpose flour a cup (140 g) at a time until the dough is too stiff to mix by hand. Turn out onto a floured board and knead in the remaining flour until the dough is smooth and satiny.

Or mix and knead all of the ingredients for a maximum of 25 minutes in a bread machine or other mixer (see page 152).

Proof the dough overnight (8 to 12 hours) at room temperature, about 70°F (21°C), in a large bowl covered with plastic wrap (or leave in the machine pan, removed from the machine, securing the plastic wrap with a rubber band). During this time, the dough should double in size in the covered bowl, or rise to the top of the machine pan. After the proof, use a spatula to gently ease the dough out onto a floured board. Allow the dough to rest for 30 minutes. If marked flattening occurs during this time, knead in additional flour before shaping.

LOAF PROOF To shape the rested dough, flatten it slightly, then lift a portion from the periphery and pull it toward the center. Continue this around the dough mass to form a rough ball (see page 34), then pat and pull into the loaf shape you desire. Place the shaped loaf on a baking sheet or in a pan and proof for 2 to 4 hours, until it doubles in bulk or nearly reaches the top of the pan. Proof for the first hour at room temperature and then at 85° to 90°F (29° to 32°C) in a proofing box.

BAKING Place the pan with its shaped, proofed loaf in a cool oven, then turn the temperature to 400°F (200°C) and bake for 55 to 65 minutes. When the loaf is baked, remove it from the pan and let cool on a wire rack for at least 15 to 20 minutes before slicing.

Pumpernickel Rye Bread

Pumpernickel is a coarsely ground rye grain with poor or no gluten, and therefore does not excel at rising. It does produce a moist, dark bread ideal for buffets. MAKES ONE 1½-POUND (680 G) LOAF

1 cup (240 ml) culture from the
  Culture Proof (page 31)
1 cup (240 ml) milk
1 teaspoon salt
2 teaspoons sugar
2 tablespoons caraway seed

1 tablespoon oil
1½ cups (170 g) coarse pumpernickel
  rye flour
2 cups (280 g) unbleached
  all-purpose flour

DOUGH PROOF Pour the culture into a mixing bowl. Add the milk, salt, sugar, caraway seed, and oil and mix. Add the rye flour and mix well. Add the all-purpose flour a cup (140 g) at a time until the dough is too stiff to mix by hand. Turn out onto a floured board and knead in the remaining flour until the dough is smooth and satiny.

Or mix and knead all of the ingredients for a maximum of 25 minutes in a bread machine or other mixer (see page 152).

Proof the dough overnight (8 to 12 hours) at room temperature, about 70°F (21°C), in a large bowl covered with plastic wrap (or leave in the machine pan, removed from the machine, securing the plastic wrap with a rubber band). During this time, the dough should double in size in the covered bowl, or rise to the top of the machine pan. After the proof, use a spatula to gently ease the dough out onto a floured board. Allow the dough to rest for 30 minutes. If marked flattening occurs during this time, knead in additional flour before shaping.

LOAF PROOF To shape the rested dough, flatten it slightly, then lift a portion from the periphery and pull it toward the center. Continue this around the dough mass to form a rough ball (see page 34), then pat and pull into an artisan-shape loaf. Place the shaped loaf on a baking sheet and proof for 2 to 4 hours, until it doubles in bulk. Proof for the first hour at room temperature and then at 85° to 90°F (29° to 32°C) in a proofing box.

BAKING Just before baking, make crisscross slashes in the dough with a razor blade. Bake in a preheated oven at 400°F (200°C) for 55 to 60 minutes. Remove it from the pan and let cool on a wire rack for at least 15 to 20 minutes before slicing.

Dark Pumpernickel Bread

This is a heavy, moist, dark bread found throughout Europe. It rises slowly and requires patience for the final proof. It is worth the wait. Pumpernickel is a coarse rye meal with bran particles. The average supermarket doesn't stock it and you may have to search in specialty sources to find it. MAKES TWO 2-POUND (900 G) LOAVES

2 cups (480 ml) culture from the
  Culture Proof (page 31)
1¹/₂ cups (360 ml) milk
2 teaspoons salt
4 teaspoons sugar

2 tablespoons oil
1 tablespoon caraway seed
¹/₂ cup (70 g) unbleached all-purpose flour
2 cups (280 g) whole wheat flour
3 cups (270 g) coarse pumpernickel flour

DOUGH PROOF Pour the culture into a mixing bowl. Add the milk, salt, sugar, oil, and caraway seed and mix. Combine the flours and add to the culture mixture, a cup at a time. When the dough becomes too stiff to mix by hand, turn out onto a floured board and knead in the remainder of the flour until the dough becomes smooth and satiny.

Proof the dough overnight (8 to 12 hours) at room temperature, about 70°F (21°C), in a large bowl covered with plastic wrap. During this time, the dough should double in size. After the proof, use a spatula to gently ease the dough out onto a floured board. Allow the dough to rest for 30 minutes. If marked flattening occurs during this time, knead in additional flour before shaping.

LOAF PROOF Divide the rested dough into 2 equal balls. Flatten each ball with your hand or a rolling pin and form an oval 1¹/₂ inches (about 4 cm) thick. Shape loaves by folding the ovals in the middle and pinching the edges together. Place the loaves on a baking sheet, seam side down, and proof for 2 to 5 hours, until doubled in bulk. Proof for the first 2 hours at room temperature and then at 85° to 90°F (29° to 32°C) in a proofing box.

BAKING Just before baking, slash the tops of the loaves in a crisscross pattern. Place the baking sheet with its shaped, proofed loaves in a cool oven, then turn the temperature to 375°F (190°C) and bake for 65 to 70 minutes. When the loaves are baked, remove them from the pan and let cool on a wire rack for at least 15 to 20 minutes before slicing.

Cinnamon Rolls

Glaze these rolls hot out of the oven with either melted butter or a mixture of confectioners' sugar, milk, and vanilla. **MAKES 12 TO 14 ROLLS**

2 cups (480 ml) culture from the
   Culture Proof (page 31)
1/2 cup (120 ml) milk
1 teaspoon vanilla extract
1 teaspoon salt
4 tablespoons (50 g) sugar
3 cups (420 g) unbleached
   all-purpose flour
2 tablespoons (30 g) melted butter
2 teaspoons ground cinnamon
1/2 cup (80 g) raisins

GLAZES
2 tablespoons (30 g) melted butter
   (optional)

1 cup (140 g) confectioners' sugar
   (optional)
4 teaspoons hot milk (optional)
1/2 teaspoon vanilla extract (optional)

DOUGH PROOF Pour the culture into a mixing bowl. Add the milk, vanilla, salt, and 2 tablespoons of the sugar and mix. Add the flour a cup (140 g) at a time until the dough becomes too stiff to mix by hand. Turn out onto a floured board and knead in the remaining flour until the dough is smooth and satiny.

Proof the dough overnight (8 to 12 hours) at room temperature, about 70°F (21°C), in a large bowl covered with plastic wrap. During this time, the dough should double in size. After the proof, use a spatula to gently ease the dough out onto a floured board. Allow the dough to rest for 30 minutes. If marked flattening occurs during this time, knead in additional flour before shaping.

LOAF PROOF Roll the rested dough into a rectangle about 1/2 inch (1.5 cm) thick. Brush the surface with the melted butter. Mix together the cinnamon and the remaining 2 tablespoons sugar, and sprinkle the sugar-cinnamon mixture and the raisins evenly over the surface of the dough. Roll up the rectangle from the long side and cut it into rolls 1 inch (2.5 cm) thick. Place the rolls close together on a baking sheet and proof for 2 to 4 hours, until the rolls have doubled in bulk. Proof for the first hour at room temperature and then at 85° to 90°F (29° to 32°C) in a proofing box.

BAKING Bake in a preheated oven at 400°F (200°C) for 25 to 30 minutes. Let cool on a wire rack; while the rolls are still hot, brush the tops with melted butter or mix together the confectioners' sugar, milk, and vanilla and drizzle with the glaze.

Salted Pretzels

Sourdough makes these basic partners for beer and spicy mustard a special treat. MAKES 15 TO
20 PRETZELS

2 cups (480 ml) culture from the
   Culture Proof (page 31)
2 tablespoons oil
1 teaspoon salt
1 tablespoon sugar

$1/2$ cup (120 ml) water
3 cups (420 g) unbleached
   all-purpose flour
$1/4$ cup (55 g) baking soda
Coarse salt

Pour the culture into a mixing bowl. Stir the oil, salt, and sugar into the water; add
to the culture and mix well. Add the flour a cup (140 g) at a time until the dough
becomes too stiff to mix by hand. Turn out onto a floured board and knead in the
remaining flour until the dough becomes smooth and satiny.

Divide the dough into 15 to 20 egg-size balls. Roll each ball into a 14-inch (35 cm)
rope by rolling between your hands. Twist and loop each rope into a pretzel shape.
Proof for 1 hour at 85°F (29°C) in a proofing box.

Add the baking soda to a large pan of water and bring to a boil. Carefully drop
the pretzels into the water one at a time. Simmer briefly, turning once. Remove them
with a slotted spoon and place on paper towels or a cloth until the water drains off.

Transfer the drained pretzels to a baking sheet. Make several oblique slashes
in the crust of each pretzel with a razor blade and sprinkle with coarse salt. Bake in
a preheated oven at 425°F (215°C) for 30 to 40 minutes, or until brown. Let cool on a
wire rack.

Caraway Crunchies

These sourdough snacks will disappear in a hurry. You can just as easily double the recipe and make two dozen. MAKES 12 CRUNCHIES

2 cups (480 ml) culture from the
   Culture Proof (page 31)
1 tablespoon (15 g) butter
1/2 cup (120 ml) milk
1 teaspoon salt
1 tablespoon sugar
3 cups (420 g) unbleached
   all-purpose flour

GLAZE
2 eggs, beaten
2 tablespoons caraway seed

Pour the culture into a mixing bowl. Melt the butter and add the milk to warm. Add the salt and sugar and stir until dissolved, then add this mixture to the culture and mix well. Add the flour a cup (140 g) at a time until the dough is too stiff to mix by hand. Turn out onto a floured board and knead in the remaining flour until smooth and satiny.

Divide the dough in half and form it into 2 balls. Roll each ball into a rectangle approximately 12 by 18 inches (30 by 45 cm). Cut the rectangles in half the long way. Cut each half into squares or rectangles and then into triangles. (The final product will be the size and shape of crescent rolls.) Brush the triangles with the beaten eggs and sprinkle with the caraway seed. Roll up the triangles from the long side and place on a baking sheet. Proof for 30 to 60 minutes at 85°F (29°C), then bake in a preheated oven at 375°F (190°C) for 20 minutes. Let cool on wire racks.

Bagels

You may think you've eaten sourdough bagels before, but unless you made them, they probably weren't the real thing. You won't forget these. MAKES 15 BAGELS

2 cups (480 ml) culture from the
  Culture Proof (page 31)
2 eggs, beaten
2 tablespoons oil
¹/₂ cup (120 ml) milk

4 tablespoons (50 g) sugar
1 teaspoon salt
3 cups (420 g) unbleached
  all-purpose flour

Pour the culture into a mixing bowl. Add the eggs, oil, milk, 2 tablespoons of the sugar, and the salt and mix. Add the flour a cup (140 g) at a time until the dough is too stiff to mix by hand. Turn out onto a floured board and knead in the remaining flour until the dough is smooth and satiny. Use additional flour if needed.

Place in a large bowl covered with plastic wrap and proof for 8 to 12 hours at room temperature, about 70°F (21°C). During this time, the dough should double in size. Gently ease the dough from the container to a floured board.

Divide the dough into 15 equal balls. Roll each ball into a 6-inch (15 cm) rope and pinch the ends together, forming a doughnut shape. Proof for 1 hour at 85°F (29°C) in a proofing box.

Bring 4 quarts (4 liters) of water to a boil and add the remaining 2 tablespoons sugar. Drop the bagels, 2 at a time, into the water. Remove them after they rise to the surface, drain on paper towels, and place on a baking sheet. Bake in a preheated 375°F (190°C) oven for 25 to 30 minutes or until brown. Let cool on wire racks.

Pizza

Pizza has been made in Italy for thousands of years. Ancient pizza napoletana was leavened by crisceto *(sourdough); a by-product of beer fermentation was used until just before the Second World War. That has since been replaced with various forms of commercial yeast. But there are ways to use natural leavening properly, as in the old days. This recipe made with sourdough culture has the original natural sourdough crust, but the toppings can be as American-style as you like. If you have Italian type 00 flour, use it; otherwise, all-purpose flour does very well. You may freeze the dough balls after the second proof; thaw it at room temperature before shaping. Traditional Italian toppings include tomato, mozzarella, and olive oil or tomato, oregano, anchovies, and olive oil.* MAKES ABOUT SIX 10-INCH (25 CM) PIZZAS

1^1/$_2$ cups (360 ml) culture from the Culture Proof (page 31)
7 cups (980 g) unbleached all-purpose or pastry flour

2^1/$_2$ cups (600 ml) water
1^1/$_2$ teaspoons salt

Mix together the culture, flour, water, and salt in a large mixing bowl and knead for at least 30 minutes to develop the gluten. Place the dough in a bowl and cover it with plastic wrap, and proof for 4 hours at 77° to 82°F (25° to 28°C) in a proofing box. Punch down and divide into 6 balls about 8 ounces (250 g) each. Place the balls on a baking sheet, cover with plastic wrap, and proof for an additional 4 hours at room temperature, about 70°F (21°C).

To form the pizzas, flatten each round by pressing on the center with the heel of your hand until a ridge begins to form at the periphery. Lift the dough by holding onto the ridge with both hands and let the weight of the dough stretch the developing circle. Turn the dough to maintain the circle, while alternately pulling on the ridge and pressing on the center until a 10-inch (25 cm) circle is formed with a ^{1}/$_4$-inch (6 mm) ridge.

Transfer the pizzas to a lightly floured baking sheet or peel and proof for ^{1}/$_2$ to 1 hour at room temperature. Sprinkle on the toppings of your choice. Bake in a pre-heated 500°F (260°C) oven, on a preheated stone if you have one, for 7 to 9 minutes, or until the edges begin to brown.

Cheese Brioche

Brioches are uniquely French creations characterized by extremely light, rich doughs. As such, brioche is hardly the most obvious use of sourdough, but try it. You may be surprised. Brioches are usually baked in special molds or straw baskets; this cheese brioche can be shaped as either a molded or braided loaf. If you don't have brioche molds, try Bundt pans.

MAKES TWO 1½-POUND (680 G) LOAVES

2 cups (480 ml) culture from the
   Culture Proof (page 31)
2 tablespoons sugar
1 teaspoon salt
4 ounces (115 g) Gruyère cheese,
   grated
4 cups (560 g) unbleached
   all-purpose flour

6 eggs
1 cup (240 g) butter

GLAZE
1 egg yolk
2 teaspoons water

Pour the culture into a mixing bowl. Add the sugar, salt, cheese, and 2 cups (280 g) of the flour and mix well.

Mix in the eggs, one at a time. Turn the dough out onto a floured board and knead in the remaining flour. The dough will be very soft and sticky at first. Knead the dough using your hands and a dough scraper until it loses its stickiness and becomes elastic, about 10 minutes. Break off walnut-size pieces of butter and, using a spatula or dough scraper, fold them, one at a time, into the dough. Knead until the dough is smooth.

Divide the dough in half and shape into 2 equal balls. Place the balls, seam side down, in brioche molds, or divide each ball into 3 and roll out each piece into a rope, then braid into 2 loaves (see page 55). Proof at room temperature, about 70°F (21°C), for 3 to 4 hours, or until doubled in bulk. Beat the egg yolk with the 2 teaspoons water and brush this glaze over the tops of the loaves. If they are in brioche molds, make 2 or 3 diagonal slashes in the tops of the brioches. Bake in a preheated oven at 400°F (200°C) for 30 minutes, or until brown. Unmold and let cool on wire racks.

Crumpets

Crumpets are as English as Big Ben. The batter is beaten vigorously to develop the gluten needed for leavening as the crumpet dough is proofed. The crumpets can be cooked free-form, like pancakes, but they are traditionally made by pouring the batter into 3- to 4-inch (8 to 10 cm) rings set on a hot griddle. Crumpet rings can be made from a can 1¹/₂ inches (4 cm) high, from which the top and bottom have been cut. They are also found on the Internet, possibly as English muffin rings. MAKES 8 CRUMPETS

2 cups (480 ml) culture from the
   Culture Proof (page 31)
¹/₄ cup (60 g) butter
¹/₂ teaspoon salt

1 egg, beaten
1 cup (140 g) unbleached
   all-purpose flour

Pour the culture into a mixing bowl. Melt the butter and stir in the salt and egg. Add this mixture to the culture and mix. Add the flour and mix well to fully develop the gluten. Cover the bowl and proof at 85°F (29°C) for 1 hour in a proofing box.

Oil a griddle and several crumpet rings. Set the rings on the griddle and pre-heat over moderate (medium-low) heat. Pour or spoon batter into the rings until they are one-third full. Cook on the griddle for 5 to 7 minutes, or until holes appear in the dough.

Remove the rings with tongs and turn the crumpets over with a spatula. Cook the opposite side for about 2 minutes. Remove to wire racks to cool a little, but eat hot if you can.

English Muffins

One winter day when the snow swirled past the windows, Jean said "I forgot to thaw any-thing from the freezer for dinner." We thought of a solution we had not prepared for years—eggs Benedict. But we didn't have English muffins. So on the spot we developed and made our first sourdough English muffins, and they were better than any we had ever tasted. Ed baked his in the oven and Jean used the griddle. The essential ingredients for eggs Benedict, in addition to those marvelous muffins (split in half), are a slice of ham, a poached egg or two, and hollandaise sauce. You can buy a packet of dry hollandaise sauce mix to simplify the preparation. We top ours with asparagus spears. MAKES 20 MUFFINS

1 cup (240 ml) culture from the
  Culture Proof (page 31)
1 cup (240 ml) water
1 cup (240 ml) milk
3 tablespoons (45 g) melted butter

2 teaspoons salt
6¹/₂ cups (910 g) unbleached
  all-purpose flour
Cornmeal for dusting

Pour the culture into a mixing bowl and stir in the water, milk, butter, and salt. Add the flour a cup (140 g) at a time until the dough is too difficult to mix by hand. Trans-fer to a floured board and knead in the remaining flour until the dough is smooth and satiny.

Divide the dough in half and form each half into a ball. Roll out each ball into an oval ¹/₂ inch (1.5 cm) thick. Use a 4-inch (10 cm) biscuit cutter to cut out 20 muf-fins. You can also use a can of the same diameter with the lid removed, or a water glass. Lightly grease two baking sheets and dust with cornmeal. Put the muffins on the prepared sheets and proof for 3 hours at room temperature, about 70°F (21°C).

Jean's method: Cook on a large electric griddle preheated to 400°F (200°C). After 2 minutes, when the bottoms are brown, reduce the heat to 325°F (165°C), turn the muffins, and cook for 8 minutes on the other side. Then turn again and cook for another 6 minutes.

Ed's method: Bake in a preheated oven at 450°F (230°C) for 7 to 8 minutes. Turn the muffins over and bake for an additional 7 to 8 minutes.

Caraway Croissant Rolls

These crescent rolls are rolled in caraway seed; you can omit these if you like. MAKES 12 ROLLS

2 cups (480 ml) culture from the
   Culture Proof (page 31)
$^1/_4$ cup (60 ml) oil
1 teaspoon salt
2 teaspoons sugar
1 egg, beaten
3$^1/_2$ cups (490 g) unbleached
   all-purpose flour

GLAZE
1 egg, beaten
2 tablespoons milk
Caraway seed

Pour the culture into a mixing bowl and stir in the oil, salt, sugar, and egg. Add the flour a cup (140 g) at a time until the dough is too stiff to mix by hand. Turn out onto a floured board and knead in the remaining flour until the dough is smooth and satiny.

Divide the dough into 2 balls. Roll each ball into a flat round about 16 inches (40 cm) in diameter and $^1/_4$ inch (6 mm) thick. Cut into triangles by first cutting each round in half, then cutting each half into thirds. Roll up each triangle from the wide end to the point.

Beat the egg together with the milk and pour some caraway seed into a shallow dish. Brush each roll with the milk-egg mixture and roll in the caraway seed. Place on an oiled or nonstick baking sheet and bend to form a crescent. When all the rolls are glazed, seeded, and formed, proof for 1 to 2 hours at room temperature, about 70°F (21°C). Bake in a preheated oven at 425°F (220°C) for 25 to 30 minutes.

Butterflake Rolls

This is a fun, buttery treat with delicious sourdough flavor. MAKES 8 TO 10 ROLLS

2 cups (480 ml) culture from the
   Culture Proof (page 31)
1/2 cup (120 ml) water
1/2 cup (120 ml) milk
1 teaspoon salt

1 tablespoon sugar
3/4 cup (180 g) melted butter
1 egg, beaten
4 cups (560 g) unbleached
   all-purpose flour

DOUGH PROOF Pour the culture into a mixing bowl. Add the water, milk, salt, sugar, half of the butter, and the beaten egg and mix. Add the flour a cup (140 g) at a time until the dough is too stiff to mix by hand. Turn out onto a floured board and knead in the remaining flour until the dough is smooth and satiny.

Proof the dough overnight (8 to 12 hours) at room temperature, about 70°F (21°C), in a large bowl covered with plastic wrap. During this time, the dough should double in size. After the proof, use a spatula to gently ease the dough out onto a floured board. Allow the dough to rest for 30 minutes. If marked flattening occurs during this time, knead in additional flour before shaping.

LOAF PROOF Roll the rested dough into a rectangle about 5 inches (12 cm) wide and 1/2 inch (1.5 cm) thick. Brush the remaining half of the butter over the dough. Cut into 4 strips lengthwise with a pizza cutter. Stack the strips with the buttered sides up. Cut the stacked strips into eight to ten 1 1/2-inch (4 cm) pieces. Put the rolls in the cups of a muffin pan with the cut sides facing down so that the layers are visible on top.

Proof for 2 to 4 hours, until doubled in bulk. Proof for the first hour at room temperature and then at 85° to 90°F (29° to 32°C) in a proofing box.

BAKING Bake in a preheated oven at 400° (200°C) for 12 to 15 minutes, or until brown. Remove the rolls from the pan and let cool on a wire rack.

Poppy Seed Rolls

When we end up with extra dough from almost anything, we'll make these rolls. MAKES
12 ROLLS

2 cups (480 ml) culture from the
   Culture Proof (page 31)
¼ cup (60 ml) oil
1 teaspoon salt
2 teaspoons sugar
1 egg, beaten
3 cups (420 g) unbleached
   all-purpose flour

GLAZE
1 egg, beaten
2 tablespoons milk
Poppy seed

Pour the culture into a mixing bowl. Add the oil, salt, sugar, and egg and mix. Add
the flour a cup (140 g) at a time until the dough is too stiff to mix by hand. Turn out
onto a floured board and knead in the remaining flour until the dough is smooth
and satiny.

Divide the dough into 12 equal balls. Form a flattened oval roll from each ball
and place on a baking sheet. Proof for 1 to 2 hours at 85°F (29°C) in a proofing box.

Beat the egg together with the milk and brush the top of each roll with the mixture; sprinkle with the poppy seed. Make a cross slash on top of each roll. Bake in
a preheated oven at 425°F (215°C) for 20 to 25 minutes, or until brown. Let cool on
a wire rack.

Parker House Rolls

This recipe makes eight to twelve Parker House rolls or, if desired, sixteen to twenty dinner rolls. For the latter, use three cups (720 ml) of culture and four cups (560 g) of flour. The rolls can be sprinkled with poppy or sesame seeds. Brush the tops with egg and sprinkle on the seeds before baking. MAKES 8 TO 12 ROLLS

2 cups (480 ml) culture from the
    Culture Proof (page 31)
3 tablespoons (45 g) melted butter
1 egg, beaten
$^1/_2$ cup (120 ml) milk

1 tablespoon sugar
1 teaspoon salt
3 cups (420 g) unbleached
    all-purpose flour

DOUGH PROOF Pour the culture into a mixing bowl. Stir in 2 tablespoons of the butter and the egg, milk, sugar, and salt. Add the flour a cup (140 g) at a time until the dough is too stiff to mix by hand. Turn out onto a floured board and knead in the remaining flour until the dough is smooth and satiny.

Proof the dough overnight (8 to 12 hours) at room temperature, about 70°F (21°C), in a large bowl covered with plastic wrap. During this time, the dough should double in size. After the proof, use a spatula to gently ease the dough out onto a floured board. Allow the dough to rest for 30 minutes. If marked flattening occurs during this time, knead in additional flour before shaping.

LOAF PROOF AND BAKING Roll the rested dough to a thickness of $^1/_2$ inch (1.5 cm) and cut into 4-inch (10 cm) rounds. With the edge of a knife, crease each round just off center. Brush lightly with the remaining butter and fold the larger part over the smaller. Place on a baking sheet and proof at 85°F (29°C) for 1 hour in a proofing box.

Or, for dinner rolls, form 16 small balls and place them side by side in an 8-inch (20 cm) square baking pan. Let them proof until they rise above the sides of the pan. Bake in a preheated oven at 375°F (190°C) for 20 to 25 minutes, or until brown.

Whole Wheat Muffins

These hearty muffins work best with a fast culture, such as our Russian culture. MAKES
12 TO 14 MUFFINS

2 cups (480 ml) culture from the
   Culture Proof (page 31)
1 egg, beaten
$1/2$ cup (120 ml) milk
1 cup (140 g) unbleached
   all-purpose flour

1 cup (140 g) whole wheat flour
2 tablespoons sugar
1 teaspoon salt
$1/4$ cup (60 g) butter

Pour the culture into a mixing bowl. Add the egg and milk and mix. In a separate bowl, mix together the flours, sugar, and salt. With a fork, cut in the butter until the mixture is finely granular. Add to the culture mixture and stir the batter until it is just moist but not lump-free.

Line a muffin tin with paper liners and spoon the batter into the cups to fill them two-thirds full. Proof at 85°F (29°C) for 1 hour. Bake in a preheated oven at 400°F (200°C) for 20 to 25 minutes, or until brown. Remove from the pan and let cool on a wire rack.

Spiced Buns

These buns are spiced inside and out—kneaded with anise seed and glazed with caraway or cumin seed. MAKES 10 BUNS

2 cups (480 ml) culture from the
   Culture Proof (page 31)
1/2 cup (120 ml) milk
1 egg, beaten
1 teaspoon salt
1 tablespoon oil
1 teaspoon crushed anise seed
1 cup (115 g) rye flour
3 cups (420 g) unbleached
   all-purpose flour

GLAZE
2 tablespoons milk
2 teaspoons caraway or cumin seed

Pour the culture into a mixing bowl. Add the milk, egg, salt, oil, and anise seed and mix. Add the rye flour and mix well. Add the white flour a cup (140 g) at a time until the dough is too stiff to mix by hand. Turn out onto a floured board and knead in the remaining flour until the dough is smooth and satiny.

Divide the dough into 10 equal balls and flatten to 1½-inch (4 cm) rounds. Place the balls on a baking sheet, brush the tops with the milk and sprinkle with the caraway or cumin seed. Proof at 85°F (29°C) for 1 to 2 hours in a proofing box. Bake in a preheated oven at 425°F (220°C) for 20 to 30 minutes, or until brown. Let cool on a wire rack.

Sourdough Biscuits

Sourdough makes marvelous biscuits. The dough is softer than bread dough, and you should mix it just enough to moisten the flour. It will be sticky and will need to be floured occasionally for handling. When cutting the biscuits, it is desirable to make a quick, sharp cut, which avoids tearing the gluten and produces better rising. If the biscuits are placed close together on the baking sheet, they will rise together and seal their adjacent cut edges.

MAKES 15 BISCUITS

1 cup (140 g) unbleached all-purpose flour
1 tablespoon sugar
$^1/_2$ teaspoon salt

1 teaspoon baking soda
$^1/_2$ cup (120 g) butter
2 cups (480 ml) culture from the Culture Proof (page 31)

In a mixing bowl, thoroughly combine the flour, sugar, salt, and baking soda. With a pastry blender or fork, cut in the butter until the mixture resembles coarse crumbs. Add the culture, stirring with a fork. The dough should be soft and moist and just pull away from the sides of the bowl. Add a little flour or milk as necessary to achieve this consistency. Turn out onto a floured board and knead briefly until the dough is soft and barely sticky. Add more flour if needed.

With a rolling pin, roll out the dough to about $^1/_2$ inch (1.5 cm) thick and cut biscuits with a 2-inch (5 cm) floured biscuit cutter. Place on a baking sheet close together and proof at 85°F (29°C) for 1 to 2 hours in a proofing box. Bake in a preheated oven at 375°F (190°C) for 20 to 25 minutes, or until golden. Serve hot.

Hamburger Buns

You won't find buns like these at a fast-food chain. Burgers served on them are truly sublime. MAKES 8 BUNS

2 cups (480 ml) culture from the
   Culture Proof (page 31)
3 tablespoons (45 g) butter
1/2 cup (120 ml) milk
2 eggs, beaten

1 teaspoon salt
2 tablespoons sugar
3 cups (420 g) unbleached
   all-purpose flour

Pour the culture into a mixing bowl. Melt the butter and add the milk, eggs, salt, and sugar. Beat with a fork to mix and add to the culture. Add the flour a cup (140 g) at a time until the dough is too stiff to mix by hand. Turn out onto a floured board and knead in the remaining flour until the dough is smooth and satiny.

Roll the dough out to a 1/2-inch (1.5 cm) thickness and cut with a 4-inch (10 cm) round cutter (a can with the top cut out works well).

Place the buns on a baking sheet and proof at 85°F (29°C) in a proofing box for 2 to 4 hours, or until doubled in bulk. Bake in a preheated oven at 350°F (175°C) for 15 to 18 minutes, or until browned. Let cool on a wire rack.

Caraway Hot Dog Buns

You can make the short conventional buns or the long ones (up to 9 or 10 inches/23 to 25 cm) by simply rolling and pulling this dough into the desired length. The sourdough caraway flavor is purely delicious! **MAKES ABOUT TWENTY 6-INCH (15 CM) BUNS**

2 cups (480 ml) culture from the
  Culture Proof (page 31)
2 tablespoons (30 g) butter
1 cup (240 ml) milk
1 cup (240 ml) water

2 teaspoons salt
1 tablespoon caraway seed
2 tablespoons sugar
6 cups (840 g) unbleached
  all-purpose flour

Pour the culture into a large mixing bowl. Melt the butter and add the milk and water to warm. Stir in the salt, caraway seed, and sugar. Add this mixture to the culture and mix well. Add the flour a cup (140 g) at a time until the dough is too stiff to mix by hand. Then turn onto a floured board and knead in the remaining flour until the dough is smooth and satiny.

Divide the dough into 20 equal pieces. Roll each piece into a rope about 6 inches (15 cm) long. Set on baking sheets and proof at 85°F (29°C) for 1 to 2 hours, or until about doubled in bulk. Bake in a preheated oven at 375°F (190°C) for 35 minutes, or until brown. Let cool on wire racks.

Breads of the Middle East

The Middle East is the cradle of sourdough. Our culture from Bahrain and two more from Egypt represent a versatile collection that goes back to the birth of sourdough. For distinctive flavors in any leavened bread, we use the culture from Saudi Arabia— though when we discovered it, it was used for flatbreads.

Our search for authentic sourdoughs challenged us to find and gain entrance to ethnic bakeries in areas where dough was saved and handed down for generations of baking. This was 1983 and some remote areas had not yet been contaminated by commercial yeast. Now they have, and the cultures we collected then are no longer available today.

As you will see, these recipes all feature the culture proof (see page 31) but the other proofs are slightly different.

Khubz Arabi

Khubz arabi *("Arab bread") is a soft, round flatbread—the pita of the desert. This is probably the most delicious pita I have ever encountered. It is produced throughout the Middle East, both commercially and in the home.* MAKES 8 FLATBREADS

2 cups (480 ml) culture from the
  Culture Proof (page 31)
1 cup (240 ml) water
1 teaspoon salt

1 tablespoon oil
5 cups (700 g) unbleached
  all-purpose flour

Pour the culture into a mixing bowl. Add the water, salt, and oil and mix. Add the flour a cup (140 g) at a time until too stiff to mix by hand. Turn out onto a floured board and knead in the remaining flour until the dough is smooth and satiny. Proof for 8 to 12 hours at room temperature, about 70°F (21°C), in a large bowl covered with plastic wrap. Then gently ease the dough from the container to a floured board.

Divide into 8 equal balls. Roll the balls into round flats about $^{1}/_{4}$ inch (6 mm) thick and form 2 stacks with the rounds, separated by paper towels. Proof the rounds at 85°F (29°C) in proofing box for about 30 minutes.

Preheat the oven and a baking sheet to 500°F (260°C). Use a hand board or large spatula to slide the rounds onto the heated baking sheet. Use care to avoid damage to the surface or the rounds may not puff completely. Bake for about 5 minutes, or until the rounds puff and start to brown. Let cool on wire racks.

Kaahk Ramazan

Kaahk, *a sort of vanilla-cinnamon cookie, are usually baked in a crescent shape, the symbol of the Ottoman Empire. They are most popular during the holy period of Ramadan and are eaten after the daily period of fasting. This is not a simple recipe, but the results are worth the effort.* MAKES ABOUT 24 CRESCENTS

2 cups (480 ml) culture from the
   Culture Proof (page 31)
2 teaspoons salt
3 tablespoons (45 g) sugar
$1/2$ cup (120 ml) warm milk
2 eggs
2 teaspoons ground cinnamon
1 teaspoon vanilla extract
4 cups (560 g) unbleached
   all-purpose flour
6 tablespoons (90 g) butter

GLAZE
1 egg, beaten
1 tablespoon sesame seeds
   or poppy seed

Pour the culture into a mixing bowl. Add the salt and sugar to the warm milk and stir to dissolve. In a separate bowl, beat the eggs and add the cinnamon and vanilla; stir in the milk mixture. Add this mixture to the culture and mix well. Add the flour a cup (140 g) at a time until the dough is too stiff to mix by hand. Turn out onto a floured board and knead in the remaining flour until the dough is smooth and satiny. Divide the dough in half and form it into 2 balls. Chill for 1 hour in the refrigerator.

Place 3 tablespoons (45 g) of the butter between 2 sheets of waxed paper and flatten with a rolling pin to an oval about 6 by 8 inches (15 by 20 cm). Roll out a second oval with the remaining butter and place both in the refrigerator to chill for 1 hour.

Turn out the chilled dough onto a floured board and roll each ball into a flattened oval about 12 by 16 inches (30 by 40 cm). Place the chilled butter in the center of each dough oval and fold the dough over the butter from all sides.

Roll the dough into a rectangle to about 12 by 16 inches (30 by 40 cm) and fold the bottom half up to the center and the top half down to the center. Repeat this rolling and folding once. Chill for 15 minutes, then roll again into a rectangle about 12 by 16 inches (30 by 40 cm). Cut the rectangle in half the long way. Then cut each half into 3 equal squares. (Sourdough is difficult to roll into an exact shape, but the objective is to form approximate squares for the next step. The size will determine the size of the finished rolls.)

Cut the squares diagonally to form triangles and roll up the triangles tightly from the broad side to the tip. Pull the triangles into crescent shapes and lightly pinch the tips together. Place the crescents on a baking sheet and proof at 85°F (29°C) in a proofing box for 1 to 2 hours, or until they have doubled in size.

Gently separate the joined tips of the crescents and brush each with the beaten egg and sprinkle with the sesame or poppy seeds. Bake in a preheated oven at 425°F (215°C) for 10 to 15 minutes, or until golden. Let cool on wire racks.

Psomi

This bread is sort of like a Greek version of French bread. Placing a pan filled with boiling water in the oven produces steam, which gives the bread a thick, chewy crust. Or try a mister: spritz the interior of the oven with water once every five minutes for fifteen minutes while the bread bakes. **MAKES TWO 2-POUND (900 G) LOAVES**

2 cups (480 ml) culture from the
   Culture Proof (page 31)
2 teaspoons salt
2 tablespoons sugar
1 tablespoon (15 g) melted butter

$^1/_2$ cup (120 ml) warm water
4 cups (560 g) unbleached
   all-purpose flour
1 tablespoon fine white cornmeal

Pour the culture into a mixing bowl. Add the salt, sugar, butter, and water and mix. Add the flour to the culture a cup (140 g) at a time until the dough is too stiff to mix by hand. Turn out onto a floured board and knead in the remaining flour until the dough is smooth and satiny. Divide the dough into 2 equal balls and form into elongated loaves. Place the loaves on a baking sheet sprinkled with the cornmeal and proof at 85°F (29°C) in a proofing box for 1 to 2 hours, or until about doubled in bulk.

Make several diagonal slashes through the tops of the loaves with a razor blade. Preheat the oven to 400°F (200°C). Immediately before baking, pour boiling water into a baking pan set on the lowest rack to create steam. Bake for 40 to 45 minutes, removing the water after the first 15 minutes. Let cool on wire racks.

Khubz with Hilbeh

Khubz is a whole wheat flatbread with a nice puff. Serve it with honey or hilbeh (see below), a fenugreek condiment widely used by the Arabs on flatbreads. Fenugreek is a somewhat bitter seed with an odor resembling celery. Search for it in ethnic food shops. MAKES TEN 4-INCH (10 CM) FLATBREADS

2 cups (480 ml) culture from the
   Culture Proof (page 31)
1 teaspoon salt

¹/₂ cup (120 ml) water
3 cups (420 g) whole wheat flour
Hilbeh (see below)

DOUGH PROOF Pour the culture into a mixing bowl. Add the salt and water and mix briefly. Add the flour a cup (140 g) at a time until the dough is too stiff to mix with a spoon. Turn out onto a floured board and knead in the remaining flour until the dough is satiny smooth.

Proof the dough overnight (8 to 12 hours) at room temperature, about 70°F (21°C), in a large bowl covered with plastic wrap. After the proof, use a spatula to gently ease the dough out onto a floured board.

LOAF PROOF AND BAKING Form the dough into 10 balls, each about 1¹/₂ inches (4 cm) in diameter. Proof at 85°F (29°C) in a proofing box for 4 hours, or until doubled in bulk. With a rolling pin, flatten the balls into 4-inch (10 cm) rounds, cover with a cloth or plastic wrap, and let rise for 30 minutes on the floured board.

Oil a heavy pan or griddle and heat until just short of smoking hot. Cook the rounds for 1 minute on each side. Serve warm with hilbeh.

HILBEH

2 teaspoons fenugreek seed
2 cloves garlic
¹/₄ cup chopped fresh cilantro

¹/₂ teaspoon salt
2 teaspoons lemon juice
1 small fresh chile, seeded

Soak the fenugreek seed in ¹/₂ cup (120 ml) cold water for 12 to 18 hours, until there is a jellylike coating on the seeds. Drain. Place all the ingredients in a blender with enough cold water to make sufficient volume to blend. Store in the refrigerator.

Saluf

This is a lightly leavened flatbread typical of most Arab breads. Its flavor comes from the eight- to twelve-hour proof. Unlike many Arab breads, this one does not puff to form a pocket. Serve warm with hilbeh (page 135). **MAKES TEN 6-INCH (15 CM) FLATBREADS**

2 cups (480 ml) culture from the
  Culture Proof (page 31)
1/2 cup (120 ml) water
1/2 teaspoon salt

1 1/2 cups (210 g) whole wheat flour
1 1/2 cups (210 g) unbleached
  all-purpose flour
Oil for brushing

Pour the culture into a mixing bowl. Add the water and salt and mix. Combine the flours, mix well, and add them a little at a time to the culture until the dough is too stiff to mix by hand. Turn out onto a floured board and knead in the remaining flour until the dough is smooth and satiny.

Proof for 8 to 12 hours at room temperature, about 70°F (21°C), in a large bowl covered with plastic wrap, until doubled in bulk. Then gently ease the dough from the container to a floured board.

Divide the dough into 10 equal balls. Flatten each ball with a rolling pin and form rounds 1/2 inch (1.5 cm) thick and 6 inches (15 cm) in diameter. Prick the surface with a fork or make holes with your fingers. Lightly brush oil on a baking sheet. Preheat the oven and the baking sheet to 550°F (290°C). Brush the tops of the rounds lightly with oil. Use a lightly floured hand board or metal spatula to transfer 2 rounds onto the heated baking sheet. Bake for 4 to 5 minutes, or until the tops are lightly brown. If the rounds tend to form a pocket, press lightly with a fork. Repeat with the remaining rounds until all are baked. Serve warm.

Khubz Saj

Khubz saj *("thin bread") is the bread of the village Arab and Bedouin. It is still prepared in the campsites with a fire of camel dung under a domed iron oven, the* saj. *By the ancient method, the thin rounds are draped over a special pillow with a hand grip on the back. When the oven is very hot, the flat round is slapped on the iron surface and removed within a minute or two.* **MAKES TWENTY-FIVE TO THIRTY 10-INCH (25 CM) FLATBREADS**

4 cups (960 ml) culture from the
   Culture Proof (page 31)
2 teaspoons salt

1 cup (240 ml) warm water
6 cups (840 g) unbleached
   all-purpose flour

Pour the culture into a mixing bowl. Add the salt and water and mix. Add the flour a cup (140 g) at a time until the dough is too stiff to mix by hand. Turn out onto a floured board and knead in the remaining flour until the dough is smooth and satiny.

Preheat the oven and a baking sheet to 450°F (230°C). Divide the dough into balls about 2 inches (5 cm) in diameter. Roll the balls into round, quite thin flats about 10 inches (25 cm) in diameter. As each flat is formed, transfer it with a hand board or spatula to the preheated baking sheet and bake for 3 minutes.

Sourdough Pancakes

Sourdough pancakes are fun and easy, if not fast. The first, twelve-hour proof provides the flavor, but they will not rise unless the yeast is fed again and given time to respond. Prospectors apparently never had that much time, and the genuine sourdough pancake is a thin, somewhat rubbery object that requires both an appetite and a certain amount of affection. So be it: there are generations of descendants from prospectors who consume rubbery pancakes and extol their virtues. You must try them for the experience and form your own opinion.

But if you can program an additional hour in the morning to give the batter a quick leavening, your pancakes will be objects of culinary art. Lacking that hour, you can achieve the same effect with a teaspoon of baking soda in 1 tablespoon of warm water added just before baking. It should be mixed in gently and the batter used immediately. Don't use more than the specified amount of baking soda or the flavor will be neutralized.

Add the flour to the other ingredients gradually until the consistency is what you want: pancakes made with a thin batter, approaching crepe consistency, or hearty, thicker ones.

Yukon Flapjacks

When you pour this batter on the griddle, have the surface piping hot. When a host of bubbles appears, it is time to turn over the cakes and brown the other side. **MAKES 12 TO 15 PANCAKES**

2 cups (480 ml) culture from the
   Culture Proof (page 31)
1 egg, beaten
2 tablespoons oil
2 tablespoons sugar

$1/2$ teaspoon salt
Unbleached all-purpose flour
   as needed
$1/2$ teaspoon baking soda (optional)

Pour the culture into a mixing bowl. Add the egg, oil, sugar, and salt and mix. Add flour to attain your desired consistency; mix until lump-free.

Proof for 1 hour at 85°F (29°C) in a proofing box. (Or, if you don't have time for this proof, dissolve the baking soda in 1 tablespoon of water and, just before cooking, gently blend with the batter.)

Heat a griddle until hot and, with a pitcher or ladle, pour 2- to 3-inch (5 to 7 cm) rounds onto the griddle. Cook for 2 to 4 minutes, turn, and cook for an additional 2 minutes. Serve hot.

Austrian Rye Pancakes

There isn't a combination of rye and sourdough that isn't good. When you're searching for something special for Sunday morning breakfast, these pancakes are what you want.

MAKES ABOUT 12 PANCAKES

2 cups (480 ml) culture from the
  Culture Proof (page 31)
1 egg, beaten
2 tablespoons (30 g) melted butter
$^1/_2$ cup (120 ml) milk

2 tablespoons sugar
1 teaspoon salt
1 cup (115 g) rye flour
Unbleached all-purpose flour as needed
$^1/_2$ teaspoon baking soda (optional)

Pour the culture into a mixing bowl. Add the egg, butter, milk, sugar, and salt and mix. Add the rye flour and then enough all-purpose flour to attain your desired pancake consistency. Mix until lump-free. Proof for 1 hour at 85°F (29°C) in a proofing box. (Or, if you don't have time for this proof, dissolve the baking soda in 1 tablespoon of water and, just before cooking, gently blend with the batter.)

Heat a griddle until hot and, with a pitcher or ladle, pour 2- to 3-inch (5 to 7 cm) rounds onto the griddle. Cook for 2 to 4 minutes, turn, and cook for an additional 2 minutes. Serve hot.

Apple Pancakes

Applesauce provides the flavor in this recipe. For a real treat, drop two peeled and cored apples into your food processor and chop them almost to a puree and substitute the puree for the applesauce. MAKES 12 TO 15 PANCAKES

2 cups (480 ml) culture from the
    Culture Proof (page 31)
1 egg, beaten
1/2 cup (120 ml) applesauce
2 tablespoons (30 g) melted butter

1 tablespoon sugar
1 teaspoon salt
Unbleached all-purpose flour as needed
1/2 teaspoon baking soda (optional)

Pour the culture into a mixing bowl. Add the egg, applesauce, butter, sugar, and salt and mix. Add flour as needed to attain your desired consistency and mix until lump-free. Proof for 1 hour at 85°F (29°C) in a proofing box. (Or, if you don't have time for this proof, dissolve the baking soda in 1 tablespoon of water and, just before cooking, gently blend with the batter.)

Heat a griddle until hot and, with a pitcher or ladle, pour 2- to 3-inch (5 to 7 cm) rounds onto the griddle. Cook for 2 to 4 minutes, turn, and cook for an additional 2 minutes. Serve hot.

Maple Pancakes

There are artificial maple flavorings, but they are not an adequate substitute for the real thing, especially in pancakes. MAKES 12 TO 15 PANCAKES

2 cups (480 ml) culture from the
    Culture Proof (page 31)
1 egg, beaten
2 tablespoons (30 g) melted butter

1/4 cup (60 ml) maple syrup
1/2 teaspoon salt
Unbleached all-purpose flour as needed
1/2 teaspoon baking soda (optional)

Pour the culture into a mixing bowl. Add the egg, butter, maple syrup, and salt and mix. Add flour to attain your desired consistency and mix until lump-free.

Proof for 1 hour at 85°F (29°C) in a proofing box. (Or, if you don't have time for this proof, dissolve the baking soda in 1 tablespoon of water and, just before cooking, gently blend with the batter.)

Heat a griddle until hot and, with a pitcher or ladle, pour 2- to 3-inch (5 to 7 cm) rounds onto the griddle. Cook for 2 to 4 minutes, turn, and cook for an additional 2 minutes.

Yukon Sourdough Waffles

These waffles will be lighter if you proof the batter for an hour at 85°F (29°C) just before adding the beaten egg whites. **MAKES 3 OR 4 WAFFLES**

2 cups (480 ml) culture from the
    Culture Proof (page 31)
2 eggs, separated
1/4 cup (60 ml) milk
2 tablespoons (30 g) melted butter

1 tablespoon sugar
1 teaspoon salt
1/2 to 1 cup (70 to 140 g) unbleached
    all-purpose flour

Combine the culture, egg yolks, milk, butter, sugar, and salt in a mixing bowl and mix briefly. Add enough flour to attain a pourable consistency and mix until lump-free. Proof for 1 hour at 85°F (29°C) in a proofing box.

Beat the egg whites to a soft peak and gently mix into the batter. Pour the batter onto a preheated waffle iron and cook for 7 to 8 minutes.

Sourdough Waffles

Sourdough waffles combine the unequaled flavor of the culture with the light texture of all good waffles. To achieve the latter, separate the eggs and beat the whites to the soft-peak stage. At the very last, just before baking, gently fold the whites into the batter. Oil and preheat the waffle iron before pouring on the batter. Use the amount of flour that gives a consistency that can be poured onto the waffle iron. Some experimentation may be necessary so the waffles are not so thin that they run over the edge of the waffle iron, but not so thick they do not cook properly.

Rye Waffles

It's hard to say whether rye waffles are better than rye pancakes until you've tried them both. Twice! MAKES 3 WAFFLES

2 cups (480 ml) culture from the
  Culture Proof (page 31)
2 eggs, separated
1/2 cup (120 ml) milk
2 tablespoons oil
2 teaspoons sugar

1 teaspoon salt
1/2 cup (55 g) rye flour
1/2 cup (70 g) unbleached all-purpose
  flour or as needed
1/2 teaspoon baking soda

Combine the culture, egg yolks, milk, oil, sugar, and salt in a mixing bowl and mix briefly. Add the rye flour and then enough all-purpose flour to attain a pourable consistency; mix until lump-free. Beat the egg whites to soft peaks and gently mix into the batter.

Just before cooking, dissolve the baking soda in 1 tablespoon of water and gently blend with the batter. Pour the batter onto a preheated waffle iron and cook for 7 to 8 minutes.

Ham Waffles

Ham is another of those savory ingredients that's a perfect match for sourdough. MAKES
3 WAFFLES

2 cups (480 ml) culture from the
  Culture Proof (page 31)
2 eggs, separated
1 cup (100 g) chopped ham
1/2 cup (120 ml) milk

2 tablespoons (30 g) melted butter
2 teaspoons sugar
1/2 to 1 cup (70 to 140 g) unbleached
  all-purpose flour
1/2 teaspoon baking soda

Combine the culture, egg yolks, ham, milk, butter, and sugar in a mixing bowl
and mix briefly. Add enough flour to attain a pourable consistency and mix until
lump-free.

Beat the egg whites to soft peaks and gently mix into the batter. Just before cooking, dissolve the baking soda in 1 tablespoon of water and gently blend with the batter. Pour the batter onto a preheated waffle iron and cook for 7 to 8 minutes.

Buttermilk Waffles

Buttermilk today is usually made from pasteurized skim milk to which a culture has been added to improve flavor and consistency. For a real treat, search out a country dairy and get the buttermilk that is a residue of butter churning. **MAKES 3 OR 4 WAFFLES**

2 cups (480 ml) culture from the
   Culture Proof (page 31)
2 eggs, separated
1/2 cup (120 ml) buttermilk
2 tablespoons (30 g) melted butter

2 tablespoons sugar
1 teaspoon salt
1/2 to 1 cup (70 to 140 g) unbleached
   all-purpose flour

Combine the culture with the egg yolks, buttermilk, butter, sugar, and salt in a mixing bowl and mix briefly. Add enough flour to attain a pourable consistency and mix until lump-free. Proof for 1 hour at 85°F (29°C) in a proofing box. Beat the egg whites to soft peaks and gently mix into the batter. Pour the batter onto a preheated waffle iron and cook for 7 to 8 minutes.

Gingerbread Waffles

The flavor of ginger is unique in both bread and waffles. You have missed a treat until you try both. **MAKES 3 OR 4 WAFFLES**

2 cups (480 ml) culture from the
  Culture Proof (page 31)
2 eggs, separated
$^1/_2$ cup (120 ml) milk
2 tablespoons (30 g) melted butter
2 tablespoons molasses
2 tablespoons brown sugar

1 teaspoon ground ginger
1 teaspoon ground cinnamon
1 teaspoon salt
$^1/_2$ to 1 cup (70 to 140 g) unbleached
  all-purpose flour
$^1/_2$ teaspoon baking soda

Combine the culture with the egg yolks, milk, butter, molasses, sugar, ginger, cinnamon, and salt in a mixing bowl and mix briefly. Add enough flour to attain a pourable consistency and mix until lump-free. Beat the egg whites to soft peaks and gently mix into the batter. Just before cooking, dissolve the baking soda in 1 tablespoon of water and gently blend with the batter. Pour the batter onto a preheated waffle iron and cook for 7 to 8 minutes.

Whole Wheat Waffles

You may need extra all-purpose flour to get the ideal waffle texture in this recipe. MAKES
3 OR 4 WAFFLES

2 cups (480 ml) culture from the
    Culture Proof (page 31)
2 eggs, separated
$^1/_2$ cup (120 ml) milk
2 tablespoons (30 g) melted butter
2 teaspoons sugar

1 teaspoon salt
$^1/_2$ cup (70 g) whole wheat flour
$^1/_2$ cup (70 g) unbleached all-purpose
    flour or as needed
$^1/_2$ teaspoon baking soda

Combine the culture with the egg yolks, milk, butter, sugar, and salt in a mixing
bowl and mix briefly. Add the whole wheat flour. Add enough all-purpose flour to
attain a pourable consistency and mix until lump-free. Beat the egg whites to soft
peaks and gently mix into the batter. Just before cooking, dissolve the baking soda
in 1 tablespoon of water and gently blend with the batter. Pour the batter onto a
preheated waffle iron and cook for 7 to 8 minutes.

Sour Cream Waffles

Does sour cream make sourdough more sour? A little: we think you'll enjoy the tang.

MAKES 3 WAFFLES

2 cups (480 ml) culture from the
   Culture Proof (page 31)
2 eggs, separated
1 cup (240 g) sour cream
2 teaspoons sugar

1 teaspoon salt
$^1/_2$ to 1 cup (70 to 140 g) unbleached
   all-purpose flour
$^1/_2$ teaspoon baking soda

Combine the culture with the egg yolks, sour cream, sugar, and salt in a mixing bowl and mix briefly. Add enough flour to attain a pourable consistency and mix until lump-free. Beat the egg whites to soft peaks and gently mix into the batter. Just before cooking, dissolve the baking soda in 1 tablespoon of water and gently blend with the batter. Pour the batter onto a preheated waffle iron and cook for 7 to 8 minutes.

Blueberry Waffles

Use fresh blueberries if possible, but frozen berries are a good second choice. MAKES 3 OR 4 WAFFLES

2 cups (480 ml) culture from the
  Culture Proof (page 31)
1 cup (150 g) fresh or frozen blueberries
2 eggs, separated
2 tablespoons (30 g) melted butter

2 teaspoons sugar
1 teaspoon salt
$^1/_2$ to 1 cup (70 to 140 g) unbleached
  all-purpose flour
$^1/_2$ teaspoon baking soda

Combine the culture with the blueberries, egg yolks, butter, sugar, and salt in a mixing bowl and mix briefly. Add enough flour to attain a pourable consistency and mix until lump-free. Beat the egg whites to soft peaks and gently mix into the batter. Just before cooking, dissolve the baking soda in 1 tablespoon of water and gently blend with the batter. Pour the batter onto a preheated waffle iron and cook for 7 to 8 minutes.

Baking Sourdoughs with Bread Machines

THERE ARE MANY home baking machines (bread machines) on the market but none currently available are designed specifically for sourdoughs. We have several of the Breadman Ultimate TR2200C, which has a bake-only cycle, but it is our impression that this machine, unfortunately, is no longer being produced. The bake-only cycle permits the user to allow the dough to ferment until it appears ready to bake and then the user, not the machine, makes the decision to bake. A used Breadman with the bake-only cycle appears occasionally on Amazon. Some machines advertise a cycle for building a sourdough starter, which seems of doubtful value. We are not as familiar with the Zogirushi S-15, but from our limited experience and what sourdough bakers tell us, its program can be used to bake sourdoughs. The critical factor is the ability of the machine to start the bake cycle without going through a mixing or kneading cycle. It must simply start to bake when the button is pushed.

The flavor of sourdough breads made in the machine is exceptional. But the time required for developing this flavor is the same as with traditional baking methods. When started with an active culture, the fermentation by which lactobacilli produce the sourdough flavor takes approximately eight hours. We call this the culture proof (see page 31). It is followed by a dough proof of eight to twelve hours to further develop the flavor and increase the activity of the wild yeast, and a loaf proof of two to four hours to ensure rising. It doesn't matter whether the baker does everything by hand or with the help of a machine: authentic sourdough still requires the fermentation of these three proofs.

A versatile way to use bread machines is to mix the ingredients in the machine and leave them in it for the culture proof and the dough proof. Then shape and proof the loaf out of the machine and bake in a conventional oven. With this method, you can use any culture and almost any machine, regardless of its idiosyncrasies, and expect to have better sourdoughs than you can buy.

Many of the recipes in this chapter are adaptations of recipes from chapter 4, with instructions for proofing and baking entirely in the machine. Note that you may need to add a little more flour or water than is called for in the ingredients list to achieve the proper dough consistency (see page 32).

To make sourdough in a bread machine, follow the steps outlined on pages 30 to 32 to fully activate and proof your culture.

Then, for the dough proof, add the proofed culture to the bread machine with the additional ingredients in the recipe and mix to knead for a maximum of twenty-five minutes, or until the dough has achieved the right consistency.

Correct dough consistency is critical for success with sourdoughs in a machine. It is a particular problem with sourdoughs, because one is never precisely sure how much flour and water come into the mix along with the culture. If the dough is too thin, it will often rise well and then collapse. If it's too thick, it may not rise as well. The problem is fairly easy to correct providing you recognize it at the start of the knead cycle and add a little additional water or flour, whichever is indicated. The trick is to watch the kneading paddle. After the dough has been kneading for three or four minutes and all the ingredients are well mixed, it should form a soft ball that catches and drags on the sides of the pan as the paddle revolves. If it forms a firm ball that revolves with or on the paddle and doesn't catch on the sides, it is too thick and isn't kneading properly. Water should be added a tablespoon at a time until the dough begins to adhere to the sides. If it doesn't form a ball, it is too thin and flour should be added a tablespoon at a time. Allow sufficient time between adding either flour or water for the flour or water to be assimilated by the dough before adding more.

After the dough is kneaded to a smooth, satiny consistency, take the machine pan out of the machine and cover it with plastic wrap secured by a rubber band. Proof the dough overnight (eight to twelve hours) at room temperature; it should rise above the top of the machine pan.

There are two ways to go from here: either bake the bread in the machine, or take the proofed dough out of the machine, shape it, and bake it in your oven.

To bake it in the machine, return the pan to the machine after the dough proof and "punch it down" by mixing for approximately one minute. You can remove the paddle after this mixing, but leave the dough in the machine pan. After the short "punching down" mix, allow the dough to rise in the machine until it again comes to the top of the pan, two to four hours. Then start the bake-only cycle, baking at 375°F (190°C) for 70 minutes.

To bake in a conventional oven, see chapter 3 for guidance on shaping and proofing the loaves and baking them.

Basic Bread

This is a universal and basic white bread available around the world. It has probably been baked with all known sourdough cultures. **MAKES ONE 1½-POUND (680 G) LOAF**

1 cup (240 ml) culture from the
Culture Proof (page 31)
1 cup (240 ml) warm water, plus
more as needed

1 teaspoon salt
3½ cups (490 g) unbleached all-purpose
flour, plus more as needed

DOUGH PROOF Mix (knead) all the ingredients for a maximum of 25 minutes in the bread machine, until the dough is smooth and satiny. Watch the dough form for the first 3 or 4 minutes and adjust the consistency as needed with additional water or flour, added 1 tablespoon at a time.

Proof the dough overnight (8 to 12 hours) at room temperature, about 70°F (21°C), in the machine pan (taken out of the machine and covered with plastic wrap secured by a rubber band). It should rise to the top of the machine pan.

LOAF PROOF AND BAKING To bake in the machine, mix the proofed dough for 30 seconds and allow it to rise in the machine for 2 to 4 hours, until it again comes to the top of the pan. Start the bake-only cycle and bake for the time programmed in the machine for white bread.

To bake in the oven, knead the proofed dough for 1 minute in the machine to form a ball. Gently transfer it to a floured board, let rest for 30 minutes, and shape first into a ball and then into the desired loaf shape. Place the shaped loaf, seam side down, in a bread pan or on a baking sheet, and proof for 2 to 4 hours, until it reaches nearly to the top of the pan or doubles in bulk. Proof for the first hour at room temperature then at 85° to 90°F (29° to 32°C) in a proofing box.

Put the pan in a cold oven, then turn the temperature to 375°F (190°C) and bake for 70 minutes. When the loaf is baked, remove it from the pan and let cool on a wire rack.

Light Swedish Limpa

Limpas are rye breads made with brown sugar or molasses. The addition of gluten produces a lighter bread. MAKES ONE 1½-POUND (680 G) LOAF

1 cup (240 ml) culture from the
 Culture Proof (page 31)
1 cup (240 ml) water, plus more
 as needed
Grated zest of 1 orange
2 teaspoons vegetable oil
¼ cup (60 g) brown sugar

1 teaspoon salt
2 teaspoons caraway seed
2 teaspoons fennel seed
1 cup (110 g) medium rye flour
2½ cups (350 g) unbleached all-purpose
 flour, plus more as needed

DOUGH PROOF Mix (knead) all the ingredients for a maximum of 25 minutes in the bread machine, until the dough is smooth and satiny. Watch the dough form for the first 3 or 4 minutes and adjust the consistency as needed with more water or flour, added 1 tablespoon at a time.

Proof the dough overnight (8 to 12 hours) at room temperature, about 70°F (21°C), in the machine pan (taken out of the machine and covered with plastic wrap secured by a rubber band). It should rise to the top of the machine pan.

LOAF PROOF AND BAKING To bake in the machine, mix the proofed dough for 30 seconds and allow it to rise in the machine for 2 to 4 hours, until it again comes to the top of the pan. Start the bake-only cycle and bake for the time programmed in the machine for white bread.

To bake in the oven, knead the proofed dough in the machine for 1 minute to form a ball. Gently transfer it to a floured board, let rest for 30 minutes, and shape first into a ball and then into a loaf. Place the shaped loaf, seam side down, in a bread pan or on a baking sheet and proof for 2 to 4 hours, until it reaches nearly to the top of the pan or doubles in bulk. Proof for the first hour at room temperature and then at 85° to 90°F (29° to 32°C) in a proofing box.

Put the pan in a cold oven, then turn the temperature to 375°F (190°C) and bake for 70 minutes. When the loaf is baked, remove it from the pan and let cool on a wire rack.

Tanya's Peasant Black Bread

Every baker should try this. The heavy rye and whole wheat flours produce a firm, heavy loaf, while the coriander and molasses complement the sourdough flavor. MAKES ONE 1½-POUND (680 G) LOAF

1 cup (240 ml) culture from the
    Culture Proof (page 31)
1 tablespoon dark molasses
1 cup (240 ml) warm milk, plus
    more as needed
1 tablespoon sugar

½ teaspoon ground coriander
1 teaspoon salt
1 cup (115 g) rye flour
1 cup (140 g) whole wheat flour
1½ cups (210 g) unbleached all-purpose
    flour, plus more as needed

DOUGH PROOF Mix (knead) all the ingredients for a maximum of 25 minutes in the bread machine, until the dough is smooth and satiny. Watch the dough form for the first 3 or 4 minutes and adjust its consistency as needed with more milk or flour, added 1 tablespoon at a time.

Proof the dough overnight (8 to 12 hours) at room temperature, about 70°F (21°C), in the machine pan (taken out of the machine and covered with plastic wrap secured by a rubber band). It should rise to the top of the machine pan.

LOAF PROOF AND BAKING To bake in the machine, mix the proofed dough for 30 seconds and allow it to rise in the machine for 2 to 4 hours, until it again comes to the top of the pan. Start the bake-only cycle and bake for the time programmed in the machine for white bread.

To bake in the oven, knead the proofed dough in the machine for 1 minute to form a ball. Gently transfer it to a floured board, let rest for 30 minutes, and shape first into a ball and then into a loaf. Place the shaped loaf, seam side down, in a bread pan or on a baking sheet and proof for 2 to 4 hours, until it reaches nearly to the top of the pan or doubles in bulk. Proof for the first hour at room temperature and then at 85° to 90°F (29° to 32°C) in a proofing box.

Put the pan in a cold oven, then turn the temperature to 375°F (190°C) and bake for 70 minutes. When the loaf is baked, remove it from the pan and let cool on a wire rack.

Anise Rye Bread

Anise and rye blend surprisingly well with sourdough in this unusual recipe. MAKES ONE
1¹/₂-POUND (680 G) LOAF

1 cup (240 ml) culture from the
Culture Proof (page 31)
1 cup (240 ml) water, plus more
as needed
1 teaspoon salt
1 tablespoon sugar

2 teaspoons ground anise
1 tablespoon vegetable oil
2 teaspoons Vital Glutens (see page 23)
1 cup (115 g) rye flour
2¹/₂ cups (350 g) unbleached all-purpose
flour, plus more as needed

DOUGH PROOF Mix (knead) all the ingredients for a maximum of 25 minutes in the
bread machine, until the dough is smooth and satiny. Watch the dough form for the
first 3 or 4 minutes and adjust the consistency as needed with more water or flour,
added 1 tablespoon at a time.

Proof the dough overnight (8 to 12 hours) at room temperature, about 70°F (21°C),
in the machine pan (taken out of the machine and covered with plastic wrap secured
by a rubber band). It should rise to the top of the machine pan.

LOAF PROOF AND BAKING To bake in the machine, mix the proofed dough for
30 seconds and allow it to rise in the machine for 2 to 4 hours, until it again comes to
the top of the pan. Start the bake-only cycle and bake for the time programmed in
the machine for white bread.

To bake in the oven, knead the proofed dough in the machine for 1 minute to
form a ball. Gently transfer it to a floured board, let rest for 30 minutes, and shape
first into a ball and then into a loaf. Place the shaped loaf, seam side down, in a bread
pan or on a baking sheet and proof for 2 to 4 hours, until it reaches nearly to the top
of the pan or doubles in bulk. Proof for the first hour at room temperature and then
at 85° to 90°F (29° to 32°C) in a proofing box.

Put the pan in a cold oven, then turn the temperature to 375°F (190°C) and bake
for 70 minutes. When the loaf is baked, remove it from the pan and let cool on a
wire rack.

Caraway Rye Bread

Rye, caraway, and sourdough is a wonderful combination. **MAKES ONE 1¹/₂-POUND (680 G) LOAF**

1 cup (240 ml) culture from the
Culture Proof (page 31)
1 cup (240 ml) water, plus more
as needed
1 teaspoon salt

1 tablespoon caraway seed
1 cup (115 g) rye flour
2¹/₂ cups (350 g) unbleached all-purpose
flour, plus more as needed

DOUGH PROOF Mix (knead) all the ingredients for a maximum of 25 minutes in the bread machine, until the dough is smooth and satiny. Watch the dough form for the first 3 or 4 minutes and adjust the consistency as needed with more water or flour, added 1 tablespoon at a time.

Proof the dough overnight (8 to 12 hours) at room temperature, about 70°F (21°C), in the machine pan (taken out of the machine and covered with plastic wrap secured by a rubber band). It should rise to the top of the machine pan.

LOAF PROOF AND BAKING To bake in the machine, mix the proofed dough for 30 seconds and allow it to rise in the machine for 2 to 4 hours, until it again comes to the top of the pan. Start the bake-only cycle and bake for the time programmed in the machine for white bread.

To bake in the oven, knead the proofed dough in the machine for 1 minute to form a ball. Gently transfer it to a floured board, let rest for 30 minutes, and shape first into a ball and then into a loaf. Place the shaped loaf, seam side down, in a bread pan or on a baking sheet and proof for 2 to 4 hours, until it reaches nearly to the top of the pan or doubles in bulk. Proof for the first hour at room temperature and then at 85° to 90°F (29° to 32°C) in a proofing box.

Put the pan in a cold oven, then turn the temperature to 375°F (190°C) and bake for 70 minutes. When the loaf is baked, remove it from the pan and let cool on a wire rack.

Cheese-Onion Bread

This is a real challenge to bake but well worth the effort of learning the secret. Both the cheese and onions add moisture. During the initial kneading, the dough appears far too stiff. As kneading and resting occur, moisture will be drawn from the onions, and the cheese will begin to melt. The true consistency becomes apparent later than with other recipes. While the second knead is in progress, evaluate the consistency. It may be necessary to mix the onions and cheese into the culture by hand—I turn off the machine and use a rubber spatula to break up the ingredients, then restart the machine mixing. MAKES ONE 1½-POUND (680 G) LOAF

1 cup (240 ml) culture from the
    Culture Proof (page 31)
½ cup (75 g) chopped onions
½ cup (60 g) grated cheese

1 tablespoon vegetable oil
1 teaspoon salt
3½ cups (490 g) unbleached all-purpose
    flour, plus more as needed

DOUGH PROOF Mix (knead) all the ingredients for a maximum of 25 minutes in the bread machine, until the dough is smooth and satiny. Watch the dough form for the first 3 or 4 minutes and adjust the consistency as needed with more water or flour, added 1 tablespoon at a time.

Proof the dough overnight (8 to 12 hours) at room temperature, about 70°F (21°C), in the machine pan (taken out of the machine and covered with plastic wrap secured by a rubber band). It should rise to the top of the machine pan.

LOAF PROOF AND BAKING To bake in the machine, mix the proofed dough for 30 seconds, or more if the consistency must be adjusted. Allow it to rise in the machine for 2 to 4 hours, until it again comes to the top of the pan. Start the bake-only cycle and bake for the time programmed in the machine for white bread.

To bake in the oven, knead the proofed dough in the machine for 1 minute to form a ball; adjust the consistency if necessary with more water or flour. Gently transfer the dough to a floured board, let rest for 30 minutes, and shape first into a ball and then into a loaf. Place the shaped loaf, seam side down, in a bread pan or on a baking sheet and proof for 2 to 4 hours, until it reaches nearly to the top of the pan or doubles in bulk. Proof for the first hour at room temperature and then at 85° to 90°F (29° to 32°C) in a proofing box.

Put the pan in a cold oven, then turn the temperature to 375°F (190°C) and bake for 70 minutes. When the loaf is baked, remove it from the pan and let cool on a wire rack.

Saudi Date Bread

We were a little apprehensive at the heavy load of dates and nuts in this recipe but when we tested it, it rose beautifully in the machine and stayed there. You can buy dates that are already chopped and save some time. MAKES ONE 1¹/₂-POUND (680 G) LOAF

1 cup (240 ml) culture from the
    Culture Proof (page 31)
¹/₄ cup (50 g) sugar
1 cup (240 ml) water, plus more
    as needed
2 tablespoons olive oil

1 teaspoon salt
1 cup (150 g) chopped dates
1 cup (100 g) chopped walnuts
3¹/₂ cups (490 g) unbleached all-purpose
    flour, plus more as needed

DOUGH PROOF Mix (knead) all the ingredients for a maximum of 25 minutes in the bread machine, until the dough is smooth and satiny. Watch the dough form for the first 3 or 4 minutes and adjust the consistency as needed with more water or flour, added 1 tablespoon at a time.

Proof the dough overnight (8 to 12 hours) at room temperature, about 70°F (21°C), in the machine pan (taken out of the machine and covered with plastic wrap secured by a rubber band). It should rise to the top of the machine pan.

LOAF PROOF AND BAKING To bake in the machine, mix the proofed dough for 30 seconds and allow it to rise in the machine for 2 to 4 hours, until it again comes to the top of the pan. Start the bake-only cycle and bake for the time programmed in the machine for white bread.

To bake in the oven, knead the proofed dough in the machine for 1 minute to form a ball. Gently transfer it to a floured board, let rest for 30 minutes, and shape first into a ball and then into a loaf. Place the shaped loaf, seam side down, in a bread pan or on a baking sheet and proof for 2 to 4 hours, until it reaches nearly to the top of the pan or doubles in bulk. Proof for the first hour at room temperature and then at 85° to 90°F (29° to 32°C) in a proofing box.

Put the pan in a cold oven, then turn the temperature to 375°F (190°C) and bake for 70 minutes. When the loaf is baked, remove it from the pan and let cool on a wire rack.

Oatmeal Bread

The rolled oats increase the fiber content of this white bread, much as whole wheat flour would. We used regular rolled oats in this recipe, but you can substitute the quick-cooking types as well. MAKES ONE 1½-POUND (680 G) LOAF

1 cup (240 ml) culture from the
  Culture Proof (page 31)
1½ cups (360 ml) water, plus
  more as needed
1 teaspoon salt

2 tablespoons brown sugar
1½ cups (170 g) rolled oats
3½ cups (490 g) unbleached all-purpose
  flour, plus more as needed

DOUGH PROOF Mix (knead) all the ingredients for a maximum of 25 minutes in the bread machine, until the dough is smooth and satiny. Watch the dough form for the first 3 or 4 minutes and adjust the consistency as needed with more water or flour, added 1 tablespoon at a time.

Proof the dough overnight (8 to 12 hours) at room temperature, about 70°F (21°C), in the machine pan (taken out of the machine and covered with plastic wrap secured by a rubber band). It should rise to the top of the machine pan.

LOAF PROOF AND BAKING To bake in the machine, mix the proofed dough for 30 seconds and allow it to rise in the machine for 2 to 4 hours, until it again comes to the top of the pan. Start the bake-only cycle and bake for the time programmed in the machine for white bread.

To bake in the oven, knead the proofed dough in the machine for 1 minute to form a ball. Gently transfer it to a floured board, let rest for 30 minutes, and shape first into a ball and then into a loaf. Place the shaped loaf, seam side down, in a bread pan or on a baking sheet and proof for 2 to 4 hours, until it reaches nearly to the top of the pan or doubles in bulk. Proof for the first hour at room temperature and then at 85° to 90°F (29° to 32°C) in a proofing box.

Put the pan in a cold oven, then turn the temperature to 375°F (190°C) and bake for 70 minutes. When the loaf is baked, remove it from the pan and let cool on a wire rack.

Sour Cream Rye Bread

This Austrian recipe is a great combination of flavors and is easy to make in any machine.

MAKES ONE 1½-POUND (680 G) LOAF

1 cup (240 ml) culture from the
   Culture Proof (page 31)
1½ teaspoons salt
2 tablespoons sugar
1 tablespoon vegetable oil

1½ cups (360 g) sour cream
1 tablespoon caraway seed
1½ cups (170 g) rye flour
2 cups (280 g) unbleached all-purpose
   flour, plus more as needed

DOUGH PROOF Mix (knead) all the ingredients for a maximum of 25 minutes in the bread machine, until the dough is smooth and satiny. Watch the dough form for the first 3 or 4 minutes and adjust the consistency as needed with more water or flour, added 1 tablespoon at a time.

Proof the dough overnight (8 to 12 hours) at room temperature, about 70°F (21°C), in the machine pan (taken out of the machine and covered with plastic wrap secured by a rubber band). It should rise to the top of the machine pan.

LOAF PROOF AND BAKING To bake in the machine, mix the proofed dough for 30 seconds and allow it to rise in the machine for 2 to 4 hours, until it again comes to the top of the pan. Start the bake-only cycle and bake for the time programmed in the machine for white bread.

To bake in the oven, knead the proofed dough in the machine for 1 minute to form a ball. Gently transfer it to a floured board, let rest for 30 minutes, and shape first into a ball and then into a loaf. Place the shaped loaf, seam side down, in a bread pan or on a baking sheet and proof for 2 to 4 hours, until it reaches nearly to the top of the pan or doubles in bulk. Proof for the first hour at room temperature and then at 85° to 90°F (29° to 32°C) in a proofing box.

Put the pan in a cold oven, then turn the temperature to 375°F (190°C) and bake for 70 minutes. When the loaf is baked, remove it from the pan and let cool on a wire rack.

Sunflower Bread

This recipe produces a light-textured yet dark and nutty bread. Use raw sunflower seeds, not roasted, for best results. MAKES ONE 1¹/₂-POUND (680 G) LOAF

1 cup (240 ml) culture from the
  Culture Proof (page 31)
1 cup (240 ml) milk, plus more as
  needed
1 teaspoon salt
1 tablespoon honey

1 tablespoon (15 g) melted butter
¹/₂ cup (50 g) raw sunflower seeds
1¹/₂ cups (210 g) whole wheat flour
1¹/₂ cups (210 g) unbleached all-purpose
  flour, plus more as needed

DOUGH PROOF Mix (knead) all the ingredients for a maximum of 25 minutes in the bread machine, until the dough is smooth and satiny. Watch the dough form for the first 3 or 4 minutes and adjust the consistency as needed with more milk or flour, added 1 tablespoon at a time.

Proof the dough overnight (8 to 12 hours) at room temperature, about 70°F (21°C), in the machine pan (taken out of the machine and covered with plastic wrap secured by a rubber band). It should rise to the top of the machine pan.

LOAF PROOF AND BAKING To bake in the machine, mix the proofed dough for 30 seconds and allow it to rise in the machine for 2 to 4 hours, until it again comes to the top of the pan. Start the bake-only cycle and bake for the time programmed in the machine for white bread.

To bake in the oven, knead the proofed dough in the machine for 1 minute to form a ball. Gently transfer it to a floured board, let rest for 30 minutes, and shape first into a ball and then into a loaf. Place the shaped loaf, seam side down, in a bread pan or on a baking sheet and proof for 2 to 4 hours, until it reaches nearly to the top of the pan or doubles in bulk. Proof for the first hour at room temperature and then at 85° to 90°F (29° to 32°C) in a proofing box.

Put the pan in a cold oven, then turn the temperature to 375°F (190°C) and bake for 70 minutes. When the loaf is baked, remove it from the pan and let cool on a wire rack.

ABOUT THE AUTHORS

GROWING UP IN a conservation-minded family imbued Ed Wood with a love for wildlife, which led to a degree in fish and game management from Oregon State University. He pursued a PhD in nutrition and biology at Cornell, where he studied under Dr. Clive McCay, one of this country's foremost pioneers in nutrition research, and Dr. Peter Olafson, an equal authority in animal pathology. From Cornell, Ed joined the U.S. Fish and Wildlife Service, where he did basic research on the pathology of trout and salmon. The challenging field of pathology drew him to the University of Washington and a Doctor of Medicine degree, followed by a residency in human pathology. Along the way, he served as a consultant for studies on diseases of the Olympia oyster and cancer in trout. During all of this time, a particular class of equally unique organisms captured his imagination—the organisms of sourdough that had produced man's bread for thousands of years.

In 1983, Ed became the chairman of pathology in a new hospital for the Saudi Arabian National Guard. He and his wife, Jean, spent a couple of years near Riyadh. Knowing that the Middle East was the historic birthplace of leavened bread, they began a quest for sourdough cultures that had been passed down through generations of bakers from the beginning of civilization. Their adventures yielded a collection of sourdoughs from around the world, some dating back to antiquity.

Jean Wood graduated from Oregon State University with a degree in pharmacy, and her background in chemistry and biology led her to an interest in the microbiology of sourdoughs. When Jean and Ed returned to the United States, they brought their cultures and international sourdough recipes with them. With this collection, they formed Sourdoughs International. Four years and many baking experiments later, they produced the first of several books on the science and art of sourdough. In addition to doing much of the writing for the company's books and instruction pamphlets, Jean did all the graphics for booklet covers and packaging, and much of the test baking in their facility on their forested ranch in the mountains of Idaho. Jean passed away in October, 2010.

CULTURES FROM SOURDOUGHS INTERNATIONAL

WWW.SOURDO.COM

IT TOOK US almost twenty-five years to collect the sourdough cultures we have chosen. Each is a product of the different organisms dominant in the various areas we visited. Many represent a personal adventure with fond memories. We pass them along to you hoping you will share our passion not only to experience the taste of the world's best bread, but also to sample a tiny part of the ancient history that produced them.

From time to time, you will hear it proclaimed that when a culture is moved from one area to another, it becomes contaminated by the organisms of the new area. Don't believe a word of it. These sixteen cultures came to Idaho from all over the world. After twenty-five years of proper care, they haven't changed an iota.

As home bakers, you are the most important ingredient in success with your cultures, and if you use and care for your cultures well, you will have the same successes with them as we have enjoyed.

Original San Francisco Sourdough

In 1997, we had the good fortune to acquire the authentic San Francisco sourdough culture. Extensive research published in 1970 identified for the first time both the wild yeast that makes this sourdough bread rise and the strain of bacteria that produces its flavor. The researchers developed methods to permit commercial bakers to duplicate the process everywhere. We are now sending this same culture to home bakers. The wild yeast was originally classified as a strain of *Saccharomyces exiguus*, called *Torulopsis holmii*. It has since been reclassified as *Candida milleri* and again reclassified as *Candida humilis*. The bacteria is *Lactobacillus sanfrancisco*. The two organisms thrive in a symbiotic relationship that has protected the culture from contamination from other yeasts and bacteria for more than a century of baking. Now you can produce authentic San Francisco sourdough in your kitchen, both by hand and in home baking machines.

A booklet of special instructions for this culture is included with it to be used in conjunction with the sourdough baking information in this book.

Italian Sourdough

After searching for Italian cultures unsuccessfully for years, we were unexpectedly contacted by Marco Parante, a globally recognized expert and consultant on authentic pizza napoletana. He offered us two cultures from the Naples area. One of these cultures has been carefully guarded and is difficult to obtain, and many of our orders originate in Italy. From Marco, we have the only authentic instructions for the use of these cultures from Ischia and Camaldoli and we are the only authorized source in the United States for these cultures. They are among the best we have ever used, consistently producing fabulous breads and pizzas that are flavorful and can be quite sour. The two cultures are packaged together with Italian recipes and culture-care instructions, allowing you to bake your own traditional and authentic pizzas, ciabattas, and Italian country breads. The recipes have also been adjusted for use in bread machines without sacrificing flavor.

New Zealand Sourdough

We have two cultures from New Zealand, which we sell together. With this combination, even the novice can be an "artisan" baker.

In 2003, we acquired from Kristeva Dowling a culture that is one of the easiest and best choices for the novice sourdough baker. It has been used around the world with great success ever since. This description in an email from Krista in New Zealand insured that we would give it a try: "I captured my own sourdough almost two years ago. It is a lovely sourdough that works for everything from whole wheat, potato, sweet breads, etc. I first caught the yeast in Rotorua and it has gotten much better and mellowed in flavour."

A year later, I heard from Charles Schatz in Wellington, who describes himself as a Yank from Brooklyn. He grew up on Eastern European rye breads, and after moving to New Zealand, he captured a rye sour culture and started producing his own rye breads. This culture introduces something special, the rye sour. As far as we know, this true rye sourdough is the only one available to the home baker. We package it in coarse pumpernickel rye, and you can use it to easily produce those fabulous rye sourdough breads.

Australian Sourdough

Australian beer and wine have become favorites around the world. Now you can add to that list another unique fermented Australian product—sourdough. Just as Australian wine has its own notable qualities, this culture produces breads with a distinctive flavor and texture. It has the added benefit of being ideal for spelt and Kamut flours. We acquired it when Dianne Shoobridge from Tasmania emailed information about a culture she had collected. "Earlier this year, I was passing a local deli in Hobart and the unmistakable smell of sourdough hit me. I decided I could try sourdough. So on a misty, late summer morning, I put a spelt flour and water mix in the middle of a paddock to capture my own culture. Within three days, I had something going and I haven't looked back."

South African Sourdough

This culture was collected by Gray Handcock in Kenilworth, a suburb of Capetown. In his email correspondence with Sourdoughs International, Handcock describes the culture and its origin this way: "I have made cultures before and indeed I made my own bread for close to 5 years. For some reason, I threw the culture out and started eating 'cardboard.' However, when I started wanting flavour in my bread again, I collected this new culture. It is very flexible with regard to rising times and can create a very strongly flavoured loaf. The taste has the potential to become very powerful when fermentation is left for 8 to 10 hours. I always use pure whole wheat, no unbleached white flour. This culture is easy going and has been trained on whole wheat, and it functions with either somewhat wet or somewhat dry doughs. It rises at temperatures down to 18° Centigrade (64°F)."

This is the only sourdough culture we are aware of that leavens whole wheat better than it does white flour, and it is therefore ideal for those who grind their own flour. The flavor is truly unique, and when combined with 100 percent whole wheat flour, it yields breads with unsurpassed texture, sourness, and flavor. We have also grown it using all white flour. The nutty flavor persists and white sourdough breads made with this culture are quite different from those prepared with our other sourdough cultures.

Sourdoughs International prepares this culture in the same manner as other cultures, except that it is grown in 100 percent whole wheat flour. Its ability to leaven whole wheat doughs offers the home baker almost unlimited opportunities to experiment with different combinations of whole wheat, spelt, Kamut, and white flours. Instructions are included with this culture.

Russian Sourdough

Russian-born Tanya Bevan contacted us because her experience with American commercial breads was a culture shock, and she was desperately searching for an Old World culture. We sent her one from Finland, and soon we became better acquainted with her. At that time, she lived in Seattle and worked as a tour guide to Russia. Since she has a background in science and makes frequent trips to Russia, she seemed an ideal person to bring us a Russian culture. We asked and she brought us two!

The one we sell is from the village of Palekh two hundred miles northeast of Moscow. It is a fast-leavening culture, handles heavy Russian whole wheat doughs, and works very well in automatic home bread machines.

French Sourdough

Our French culture is from a small bakery on the outskirts of Paris that has been in business for more than 150 years. The starter rises very well and the dough has one of the mildest sourdough flavors.

Austrian Sourdough

Ed has quite a story to tell about acquiring this culture. It almost landed him in a Saudi jail. The culture is from the old section of Innsbruck and the bakery carries a sign over the entrance proclaiming 1795 as the year the business opened.

Ed says, "We were on our way from Saudi Arabia to West Germany, where I was to learn how to use the electron microscope. By pure serendipity, we had stopped by a small bakery and were staring through a window at a sign saying "Sauer Brot"! Even with no German, we knew what that meant and went inside on the hunt. Hand signals worked well enough to get us to a partially underground room with three bakers at work, and we left with a sample of dough.

"A week later, I had flattened, dried, and powdered the dough, and just before we left for Saudi Arabia, I wrapped the white powder in aluminum foil and pushed the package into a pocket of my sport jacket. I forgot all about it until we walked through a metal detector at the Jeddah airport and I was forcibly reminded. An armed guard was in my face instantly and I was searching for an explanation, any explanation. I finally introduced my dried culture as the remnants of my lunch, which didn't seem to be going over too well, when some other soul tripped the same detector and the guard waved me on."

The culture is especially adapted to rye flours, rises somewhat slowly, and produces one of the more sour doughs.

Yukon Sourdough

Our acquisition of the Yukon culture has to be the strangest story of them all. We got it when we were in Saudi Arabia. We had just arrived in a beautiful new hospital built for the Saudi Arabian National Guard and knew absolutely no one. I was walking down a corridor when someone behind me shouted, "Hey, Ed!" That shout came from a former medical school classmate, Art Harris, who was the hospital's radiologist and whom I hadn't seen in well over ten years. As we caught up, it emerged that his physician father practiced in the Yukon and had been given a culture from a local prospector. He had given some of it to his son.

I had another culture with me and the two of us decided on a baking experiment to determine if the two cultures were actually different. We did just that and the results could not have been more definitive. The flavor of the Yukon inspired us to search Europe and the Middle East for other sourdoughs, to see how they differed in their turn. The Yukon culture has a moderately sour flavor, and I have a host of friends who swear it is the only culture for real Yukon sourdough flapjacks.

Finnish Sourdough

When our son, Keith, a biochemist and avid sourdough baker, made a business trip to Finland he was programmed to bring back an authentic Finnish culture. He had to go to small villages to find one, but he did return with both a culture and a book on Finnish breads. This culture has a wonderful and distinctive flavor and it rises well.

Egyptian Sourdough: The Red Sea Culture

This culture is from one of the oldest ethnic bakeries in Egypt. We found it in Hurghada on the shore of the Red Sea, when this city was still just a village. The bread was actually placed out on the street to rise. This culture has a mild flavor and works well in home bread machines—certainly a new environment for it.

Egyptian Sourdough: The Giza Culture

I call this culture La Giza, Queen of the Pyramids. It came from an ethnic bakery in the shadow of the pyramids. Jean overcame the suspicions of the baker by making friends first with a goat tied nearby, then with a ten-year-old boy attached to the goat. It is undoubtably the same culture we captured several years later in the same area for the National Geographic Society that is said to have fed thirty thousand pyramid builders. Dough made from this culture rises very well and is moderately sour. I have used it for all the Middle Eastern breads described in this book and it does the same good job with all the other breads I have experiemented with. It is becoming increasingly popular as home bakers stumble across it. It's a sleeper and has a fascinating history.

Bahraini Sourdough

Bahrain is thought by many to be the ancient Garden of Eden. Since antiquity it has been a place where East meets West and to this day it is a curious mixture of the oldest and the newest. Our Bahrain sourdough culture is from the oldest of the old. It rises well and is one of the most sour we've encountered.

Saudi Arabian Sourdough

In the twentieth century, the Saudis completely transformed their country from a country of villages to a country of modern cities the equal of any in the world. But the desert Bedouin have survived that transformation almost unchanged. The hospital I worked in was built fifteen miles from Riyadh to supply modern medical care to the Saudi Arabian National Guard and their families. The Guard, all Bedouin, settled near the hospital and brought their shops and souks with them. One was a bakery that produced flatbreads straight from the desert. They also produce spit-roasted chicken, and the place was known by us expatriates as Chicken Charlie's. This is where we found our desert sourdough; it rises moderately well and has one of the most distinctive flavors of all the cultures.

For information on ordering these cultures, contact:
Sourdoughs International
P.O. Box 670
Cascade, ID 83611
Fax: 208-382-3129
www.sourdo.com

INDEX

C

Candida humilis, 8, 168

Caraway seeds
  Caraway Croissant Rolls, 121
  Caraway Crunchies, 115
  Caraway Hot Dog Buns, 129
  Caraway Rye Bread, 108, 158
  Caraway Spelt Bread, 100

Challah, 57–58

Cheese
  Cheese Bread, 64–65
  Cheese Brioche, 118
  Cheese-Onion Bread, 66, 159

Christmas breads
  Austrian Christmas Bread, 81
  German Christmas Bread (Stollen), 82
  Swedish Christmas Bread, 83

Cinnamon
  Cinnamon-Raisin-Nut Bread, 80
  Cinnamon Rolls, 113
  Cinnamon Spelt Rolls, 102–3

Citron, candied
  Austrian Christmas Bread, 81
  German Christmas Bread (Stollen), 82

Cranberries
  Cranberry-Blueberry Rye, 53
  Cranberry-Nut Sourdough, 52

Croissant Rolls, Caraway, 121

Crumpets, 119

Crunchies, Caraway, 115

Crust texture, 36

Culture proof, 25, 31–32

Cultures
  activating dry, 28–29
  Australian, 169
  Austrian, 171
  Bahrain, 173
  capturing, 15–16
  containers for, 29
  contamination of, 14, 15
  dried, 14–15

Egyptian, 10–11, 172
feeding, 14
Finnish, 172
French, 170
fully active, 30–31
Giza, 10–11, 172
importance of, 13
Italian, 168
New Zealand, 168–69
Original San Francisco, 167–68
proofing, 25, 31–32
Red Sea, 172
Russian, 170
Saudi Arabian, 173
from Sourdoughs International, 167–73
South African, 169–70
storing, 14
"washing," 29–30
wild, 7–10, 13
Yukon, 171–72

Currants
  German Christmas Bread (Stollen), 82

D

Dark Pumpernickel Bread, 112

Dates
  Date Bread, 51
  Saudi Date Bread, 160

Dough
  consistency of, 32, 152
  kneading, 33–34, 152
  proofing, 33
  shaping, 34

Dowling, Kristeva, 168

Durum flour, 20
  Basic Durum Bread, 93
  Durum Rye Bread, 94
  Durum Sunflower Bread, 95
  substituting, 93

Pumpernickel flour, 111, 112
  Dark Pumpernickel Bread, 112
  Pumpernickel Rye Bread, 111

Q

Quinn, Bob, 18

R

Raisins
  Austrian Christmas Bread, 81
  Cinnamon-Raisin-Nut Bread, 80
  Cinnamon Rolls, 113
  Cinnamon Spelt Rolls, 102–3
  German Christmas Bread (Stollen), 82
  Raisin Rye Bread, 105–6
  Rosemary Bread, 71
Red Sea culture, 172
Rolls
  Butterflake Rolls, 122
  Caraway Croissant Rolls, 121
  Cinnamon Rolls, 113
  Cinnamon Spelt Rolls, 102–3
  Parker House Rolls, 124
  Poppy Seed Rolls, 123
Rosemary Bread, 71
Russian culture, 170
Rye flour, 21
  Anise Rye Bread, 157
  Austrian Rye Pancakes, 140
  Austrian Spelt Bread, 99
  Austrian Wheat Rye Bread, 110
  Caraway Rye Bread, 108, 158
  Caraway Spelt Bread, 100
  Cranberry-Blueberry Rye, 53
  Durum Rye Bread, 94
  Finnish Rye Bread, 104
  German Rye Bread, 109
  German Spelt Bread, 98
  Kamut Bread, 91
  Light Swedish Limpa, 44–45, 155

Malt Beer Bread, 59–60
No-Knead German Spelt Bread, 89
No-Knead Kamut Bread, 90
Onion Bread, 67
Pumpernickel Rye Bread, 111
Raisin Rye Bread, 105–6
Rye Waffles, 144
Sour Cream Rye Bread, 107, 162
Spelt Bread, 96–97
Spiced Buns, 126
Swedish Christmas Bread, 83
Tanya's Peasant Black Bread, 46–47, 156
See also Pumpernickel flour

S

Saccharomyces cerevisiae, 2, 6–7
Salt, 23
Salted Pretzels, 114
Saluf, 136
San Francisco Sourdough, 40–41
Saudi Arabian culture, 173
Saudi Date Bread, 160
Schatz, Charles, 169
Shaping, 34
Shoobridge, Dianne, 169
Slashing, 35
Sour cream
  Sour Cream Rye Bread, 107, 162
  Sour Cream Waffles, 149
Sourdough Biscuits, 127
Sourdough breads
  crust texture of, 36
  cultures for, 13–16
  definition of, 1
  flours for, 16–23
  freezing and thawing, 36
  history of, 1–3, 5
  other ingredients in, 23–24
  See also individual recipes
South African culture, 169–70